The Marian Way of

Raphael's *Sistine Madonna* (detail)

THE MARIAN WAY
of
HEART KNOWLEDGE

❧

FROM MARY
THROUGH ST. JOHN'S GOSPEL
TO RUDOLF STEINER'S
PHILOSOPHY OF FREEDOM

NEILL REILLY

LINDISFARNE BOOKS | 2023

2023
Lindisfarne Books
An imprint of SteinerBooks/Anthroposophic Press, Inc.
P.O. Box 58, Hudson, NY, 12534

"Annunciation" by Denise Levertov, from *A Door in the Hive,*
copyright ©1989 by Denise Levertov. Reprinted by
permission of New Directions Publishing Corp.

Front cover image: *Sistine Madonna* (c. 1513–14, detail) by Raphael
(Gemäldegalerie Alte Meister, Dresden)
Back cover image: *The Pietà* (1498–99) by Michelangelo
(Basilica Papale di San Pietro, Vatican)
Design: William Jens Jensen

LIBRARY OF CONGRESS CONTROL NUMBER: 2022943343
ISBN: 978-1-58420-891-4

Printed in the United States of America

Contents

• *Foreword by J. Bruce Murphy*   ix

• *Introduction*   xix

Mary, St. John, and Dr. Rudolf Steiner   1

The Gospel of St. John   27

The Philosophy of Freedom   36

Marian Sites   48

Marian Apparitions   53

• "Our Lady of Guadalupe," by Gene Gollogly   54

• *Bibliography*   79

• *About the Author*   81

*"Mary kept all these things,
and pondered them in her heart."*

(Luke 2:19)

Dedicated to Mary

THANKS TO

J. Bruce Murphy
Andrew Linnell
Jens Jensen
Gene Gollogly
Paul O'Leary
Robert McDermot
& Charles Wick
for their enthusiastic support.

FOREWORD

J. Bruce Murphy

"…all ages to come shall call me blessed." (Luke 1:48)

In his previously published collection *Songs and Dreams*, the author of this book recorded this song at Easter in 2003.

> Consider Mary.
> Her faith allowed Me to be born.
> Her humble and meek soul absorbed My pain.
> She held My body after My death.
> She endured the worst of pains.
> She bore witness to My Resurrection.
> Follow Mary's path to Me.*

This "Song" can easily be seen as the seed from which the following book has grown and blossomed.

The Marian Way of Heart Knowledge: From Mary through St. John's Gospel to Rudolf Steiner's Philosophy of Freedom is quite a title. The ambitious undertaking in this book encompasses much. A certain level of courage is needed to attempt an exploration of the sanctity of the mysteries surrounding Mary as revealed in the Bible, and from there to proceed to a Marian Way of Heart Knowledge that leads us to discover the connections to Rudolf Steiner's *Philosophy of Freedom*. The theme of this book is to show that these holy mysteries are not allegory, poetry, or simple fantasy. Rather, they are actual facts that can be known and experienced by

---

*   Reilly, *Songs and Dreams*, p. 50.

each of us, and mere sense-bound intellect will not suffice for us to reach an understanding of these mysteries.

This exploration is not supposed to be easy. The facts of existence are by no means simple. Edward Reaugh Smith writes in his book *The Burning Bush*:

> These matters are not simple, but as he [Dr Steiner] often said, "If there are so many complex things in the world, how can we expect the most magnificent event in the entirety of evolution to be simple?"*

Mary presents herself to us as a mystery. Her story is complicated and difficult to fathom. It is especially hard for our modern way of thinking to comprehend these mysteries of Mary.

> No part of the Nativity accounts has so offended the modern thinking person as that of the Virgin Birth, the Immaculate Conception, and the Perpetual Virginity of Mary.**

Mary is known by many names and many titles. Mary is called The Blessed Mother, Holy Mother of God, Our Lady of Sorrows, Queen of Peace, Immaculate Mary, Our Lady of Perpetual Help, Virgin Mary, and Mediatrix of all Graces. There are many more titles bestowed on Mary than could be listed here. The unique and all-important role that Mary plays in the evolution of humankind is difficult for some to accept and understand.

How can we accept and understand Mary and the miracles surrounding her? Descriptions of spiritual facts are difficult for us to accept with our usual everyday thinking. In her

---

*   Smith, *The Burning Bush*, p. 69.

**   Ibid., p. 65.

book *And if He Had not Been Raised...*, Judith von Halle writes that the spiritual events she describes are no parable or pretty legend but are actual facts, even if they appear absurd. The facts are true and require of us another kind of thinking: "[This] constitutes for our present-day intellectual, or rather scientific mode of thinking, a sheer provocation."*

The two following anecdotes are just stories, but they convey the heartfelt love for Mary and the high esteem in which Mary is held by many souls.

Mary the Merciful

There is an old story about St. Peter and the Lord. In it, the Lord takes issue with the quality of Peter's performance as "Keeper of the Gates of Heaven." The Lord tells Peter that He has seen some folks in Heaven who should not be there. Peter protests: "I am doing my best. It is not my fault that Your Mother keeps letting them in the back door."

Mary, Mother of God

There is also a tale of a Baptist minister who passes on and meets his old friend Father Tom O'Leary in heaven. Father Tom says, "Reverend Bob, I am so glad to see you made it." Reverend Bob answers, "There is no need to be so surprised, Tom. Jesus is a friend of mine." "Wonderful," says Father Tom. "And now, then, in that case, I'm sure you will be wanting to be introduced to His Mother."

In the attempt to further our acceptance and understanding of Mary, this book explores a Marian Way of Heart Knowledge. This call to Heart Knowledge points to another reality, or rather a way of knowing, that gives us the whole

---

* Von Halle, *And if He Had not Been Raised...*, p. 122.

of reality, not just a fractured, abstract, and illusory picture of the world.

> Our civilization is calculated to make men cognize every-thing with their heads. Ideas rest in the head as upon a couch. The ideas are at rest in the head as though they lay in bed. They are asleep; they only mean this or that. We carry them stored up in us as in so many little pigeon holes and with the rest of our being we are unconcerned with them.*

There are ways of knowing that can lead us to cognize the whole of reality, not just a mere fractured, abstract picture of the world. When the psychologist C. G. Jung was staying with the Pueblo Indians, they made a statement. They said that white Americans are "mad," and the reason they gave was that "the Americans believe they think with their brains, but we know that men think with their hearts."**

In an effort to shed light on what is meant by knowledge that is truly human—that is, imaginative and intuitive—Dr. Franz Winkler quotes Robert Ulich's *The Human Career* at length in his book *Man: The Bridge between Two Worlds.*

> First, though intuition is not the mere extension, it is by no means the negation of critical intelligence and of the laws of logic.... Second, intuition, though appearing like a "gift" and beyond the reach of mere effort, is nevertheless the result of preparation, which may be of intellectual character or other forms of self-discipline.... Paradoxically, though it may seem to speak of "trained" intuition, it is the only form which deserves its name. All other claims are on behalf of quackery.... True intuition is dedication, false intuition is intellectual self-indulgence.***

---

*   Gardner, *The Experience of Knowledge*, p. 2.

**   Morey, *Native Americans and Our Way of Life*, p. 9.

***   Winkler, *Man, The Bridge between Two Worlds*, p. 86.

In the pursuit of an understanding of Mary that is undertaken in this book, it is clear that we are dealing with events beyond the reach of our normal faculties. Without effort on our part and help of some kind, Mary remains one more unsolvable mystery, to be dismissed as just some nice myth with no reality. In our striving to be open and reverent in our devoted pursuit of knowledge of these mysteries, we begin to tread the path of the Marian Way of Heart Knowledge.

> It is not easy, at first, to believe that feelings like reverence and respect have anything to do with cognition. This is due to the fact that we are inclined to set cognition aside as a faculty by itself—one that stands in no relation to what otherwise occurs in the soul. In so thinking we do not bear in mind that it is the soul which exercises the faculty of cognition; and feelings are for the soul what food is for the body.*

Devotion, reverence, "thinking with the heart" leads not merely to understanding "about" Mary or "concepts" of Mary, but to the Marian Way of Heart Knowledge, which is an encounter with Mary in the present. It is possible to live into the events of Mary's life.

> The human being is obliged to separate himself from his sense-based thinking. What is demanded here is a "thinking with the heart."... Thinking with the heart, by the way, provides essentially more exact and more truthful results than brain-based thinking. Thinking with the heart recognizes the truth hidden behind the outward appearance.**

---

* Steiner, *Knowledge of the Higher Worlds*, pp. 12–13.

** Von Halle, *And if He Had not Been Raised...*, p. 123.

Denise Levertov's poem "Annunciation" is included in the section of this book that deals with Mary in the Bible (see page 16). The poem is itself an experience of the Marian Way of Heart Knowledge. "Annunciation" is stunning in its simplicity. By means of careful, exact, and devoted observation, the scene of the Annunciation comes powerfully to life before us. When Mary's free deed, Mary's "yes" is experienced, the profundity of Mary's acceptance is awe-inspiring. Mary's courageous and free deed opens the way for the most spiritual necessity of all evolution.

> By consciously submitting to what we recognize to be a necessity...out of our own free will we yield to necessity. There is no external pressure on the physical plane. We must follow compulsion out of inner freedom, as it were. That is to say, we become acquainted with spiritual necessity, thereby making ourselves more and more free with regard to life on the physical plane.*

Levertov's recognition of Mary's courage is moving. She names Mary "bravest of all humans" with "courage unparalleled," saying, "Compassion and intelligence fused in her, indivisible." Courage as described here is a heart virtue, an example of the Marian Way.

Mary is mentioned only a few times in the Gospels, but Mary is present at the time of the most significant events: the Annunciation, the Nativity, the Wedding at Cana, the Crucifixion, and Pentecost.

In this book, special emphasis is placed on the words of Christ to Mary and John as they stood at the foot of the Cross. Study of this special relationship "is essential to our understanding of Christ, Mary, John, Christianity, St.

---

* Steiner, *Necessity and Freedom*, p. 88.

Michael, the Gospel of St. John, Anthroposophy, and *The Philosophy of Freedom*" (page 8). It is safe to say that just about everything depends on experiencing this mystery.

> Rudolf Steiner spoke these words about the Sophianic origin of this Gospel: He [the Christ] hangs on the Cross, at his feet stand His mother and His initiated pupil whom He loved. The pupil is to bring man the wisdom [Sophia], the knowledge of the significance of Christ. This is why the Mother-Sophia is referred to with the words: "This is your mother, you must love her." The spiritualized mother of Jesus is the Gospel; she is the wisdom [Sophia] which leads men to higher knowledge. The disciple has given us the mother-Sophia; that is to say, he has written the Gospel for us.*

This book celebrates the powerful connection of Mary's world-historic deed to the thoughts expressed in *The Philosophy of Freedom,* especially in regard to Mary's openness to the Holy Spirit and Mary's courageous actions that spring from her "love for the deed." In *The Philosophy of Freedom,* we have a work in which "for the first time in humankind's history, the nature of freedom is worked out and the paths to its realization are made evident."** "Steiner's epistemology has the agenda of establishing that all humans are individually responsible and therefore free."***

In the further course of this book, we proceed to deal with the development of the Marian Way of Heart Knowledge especially in its connections to Rudolf Steiner's *The Philosophy of Freedom.* Steiner writes in his 1894 preface (revised 1918): "...in this book the aim is a philosophic

---

*   Prokofieff, *The Heavenly Sophia,* p. 125.

**   Prokofieff, *Anthroposophy and the Philosophy of Freedom,* p. 86.

***   Reif Hughes, *American Philosophy and Rudolf Steiner,* p. 242.

one...knowledge itself shall become organically alive."* Ralph Waldo Emerson had a similar insight to heartfelt knowledge:

> But when a faithful thinker, resolute to detach every object from personal relations and see it in the light of thought, shall, at the same time, kindle science with the fire of the holiest affections, then will God go forth anew into the creation.**

The necessity for this revolution in our manner of thinking is crucial to our survival. Rudolf Steiner writes in the preface to the 1918 revised edition of the *The Philosophy of Freedom*:

> An attempt is made to prove that there *is* a view of the nature of man's being which can support the rest of knowledge; and further, that this idea completely justifies the idea of free will, provided only that we have first discovered that region of the soul in which free will can unfold itself.***

Can we know the world? Are there limits to our knowing? Do we have free will? These are the questions that lie at the basis of our striving. "In this book, the attempt is made to show that a knowledge of the spirit realm *before* entering upon the actual spiritual experience is fully justified."**** The importance of the experience the reader undergoes in a study of *The Philosophy of Freedom* cannot be overstated. Wrestling with the thoughts and arguments in Steiner's book leads to a real experience of catharsis. This experience will

---

*   Steiner, *The Philosophy of Freedom*, p. xxix.

**   Emerson, *Collected Works*.

*** Steiner, *The Philosophy of Freedom*, p. xxiii.

**** Ibid., p. xxv.

contribute to establishing a secure foundation upon which we can confidently build an understanding of the human being and the world.

> [In *The Philosophy of Freedom*,] Rudolf Steiner validates a theory of cognition that applies equally to natural science as well as to spiritual science. This is why it was only on this basis that the connection between intellectuality and spirituality in anthroposophy could become possible.... This book should in no way remain merely an object of study for its readers, but should become a genuine *book of life* for all those whose heart's concern is the full realization of mankind's true destiny.*

The final chapter of this essay concerns the many Marian Sites and the numerous Marian Apparitions that have been reported. The Marian appearances at Fatima, Lourdes and Medjugorje, to name just a few, are well-known and relatively recent events. In his book *Songs and Dreams* the author wrote that *"clarity has been seduced by sloth."*** How true! Mary is present and with us now. Mary asks us to pray, to pray the Rosary and to pray for peace. Mary's plea exhorts us to be awake and active in these perilous times.

An essay describing the miraculous events surrounding Our Lady of Guadalupe and Juan Diego, written by Gene Gollogly, is included here. The story is amazing and Gene does a wonderful job of recounting the many miracles that surround this apparition of Mary. Even though the apparition occurred almost five hundred years ago, it speaks to our souls today. Gene writes that Our Lady asks Juan Diego "Where are you going?" Gollogly says, "This is a question that can be asked of all of us. Our Lady is then asking all

---

*   Prokofieff, *Anthroposophy and the Philosophy of Freedom*, p. 131.

**   Reilly, *Songs and Dreams*, p. 85.

of us to build a temple—not an outer building, but an inner sanctuary where we can meet her."* Will we awake or will we remain asleep like the disciples in the Garden of Gethsemane?

Similarly, this book, *The Marian Way of Heart Knowledge,* places the same question before our souls. Where am I going? Do I have the courage and the "love for the deed" to say yes? The answer to this question is up to each individual. There are many helpers available to us along the way to our finding the answer to this question. The study of this book is one such help. This book directs us to the greatest sources of help available to find the courage needed to make our response. What better help could we ever have than Mary, the Gospel of St. John, and *The Philosophy of Freedom?* As the "Song" quoted at the beginning of this essay exhorts, "Consider Mary.... Follow Mary's path to Me."

---

*   See page 60.

INTRODUCTION

There are many valid perspectives on life. There is a loving God and life is sacred. Life is absurd and has no rhyme or reason to it; it is "Full of sound and fury, signifying nothing."* Most of us vacillate between these and myriad other perspectives on a daily basis. We strive to make sense out of what seems to be chaos. But certain events and data points stick out and suggest more than meets the eye. Either reality doesn't make sense or our imagination is too earth bound to comprehend it. Life is so amazingly complex and beautiful, from the stars to the genetic sequencing in the wondrous bodies we inhabit, it can give one pause. One of the great mysteries we can consider is how Mary's heart knowledge of Christ influenced the understanding of John the Evangelist and all of us, up to and including Dr. Steiner's *Philosophy of Freedom*. Pondering the Marian way of heart knowledge is the thesis of this book.

I was born in Mary Immaculate Hospital in Jamaica, Queens, New York. My parents wanted their children to attend Catholic schools from kindergarten through twelfth grade. They bought a small house in Manhasset near St. Mary's Church. Our home was a hundred yards from the boys' high school, a hundred and fifty yards from the church, and two hundred yards from the grammar school and the girls' high school. We went to church and school

---

* Shakespeare, *Macbeth,* act 5, scene 5, lines 26–27.

in our own neighborhood. To say we were parochial is an understatement.

We were taught by nuns who were in The Immaculate Heart of Mary (IHM) Order. The brothers were Marist Brothers. Both orders are dedicated to Mary and teaching.

We competed in athletics with the words St. Mary on our chests. We inscribed "JMJ" (Jesus, Mary, and Joseph) at the top of each paper on which we wrote. We absorbed the colored stained-glass windows depicting Mary and the statues of her graceful demeanor and honored her with a May crowning every year.

My Irish grandmothers' Funeral Masses were celebrated in St. Mary's Church, as were those of my parents. My brother had his Memorial Service there. We celebrated my niece's Funeral Mass at St. Mary's, making her the fourth generation of our family to celebrate a Funeral Mass or Memorial Service in the Church of St. Mary. My wife and I were married in that church, as were my sister and my wife's sister. Most of my family—my wife, our children, our siblings, and their children—received major sacraments in the church: Baptism, Penance, Holy Communion, Confirmation, Marriage, and Funeral Masses. I hope my Funeral Mass will be in St. Mary's Church.

At the center of the Church, directly over the pure white marble altar where the priest celebrates transubstantiation, floats a Eucharistic Cross statue, suspended from the ceiling with two chains. The radiant rays above Christ's head proclaim that redemption has begun. Dr. Steiner stated that this is The Turning Point in Time. This Eucharistic Cross depicts the blood of Christ dripping into the soil where it fosters the growth of grapes for the wine and wheat for the communion host, demonstrating Christ's statement at The Last Supper.

And as they were eating, Jesus took bread, and blessed it, and brake it, and gave it to the disciples, and said, Take, eat; this is my body. And he took the cup, and gave thanks, and gave it to them, saying, Drink ye all of it; For this is my blood of the new testament, which is shed for many for the remission of sins. (Matt. 26:26–28)

The crucified Christ is on the cross, with Mary and John the Evangelist on either side. The centrality of Mary is most evident.

St. Mary's Church has stained-glass windows portraying critical points in Mary's life, such as Pentecost and apparitions at Fatima, Lourdes, and Guadalupe (see next page).

While walking around the stained-glass windows, one can enter their mood of reverence. The Eucharistic Cross over the altar dominates the scene and the mood.

A study of Mary, the most amazing woman ever born, seems appropriate.

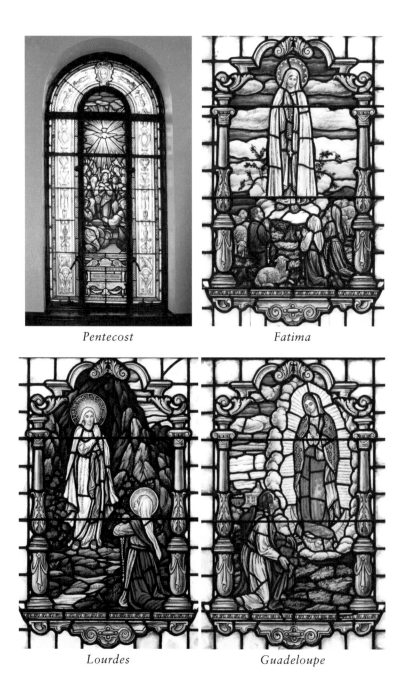

Pentecost

Fatima

Lourdes

Guadeloupe

MARY, ST. JOHN, AND DR. RUDOLF STEINER

This book makes constant references to Dr. Steiner's books and lectures. Whereas it helps to be familiar with his thoughts, it is not necessary. For those unfamiliar with his thinking, there is a vast portfolio of three hundred and fifty volumes. He delivered more than six thousand lectures. At the core of Steiner's work is the "Mystery of Golgotha," which includes Christ's Passion, but even more important, His Resurrection. Steiner stated that the Mystery of Golgotha is the "Turning Point in Time" for humanity and the world. Note the use of the present tense. The Turning Point in Time is not a singular, historic moment; it is in the present tense and ongoing—i.e., it is eternal. Steiner completely agreed with St. Paul's statement, "And if Christ be not risen, then is our preaching vain, and your faith is also vain" (1 Cor. 15:14, KJV). Steiner stated that modern humanity can have the Pauline experience on the way to Damascus. The second coming of Christ can be experienced now in the present tense. Otherwise, what is the meaning of this statement of Christ? "I am with you always, even unto the end of the world. Amen" (Matt. 28:20).

Dr. Steiner called his work "Anthroposophy." He took the critical approach of the scientific method, but did not limit it to materialistic existence. He applied rigorous scientific methods of observation, hypothesis, testing, and repeating the process to spiritual matters. The key to Steiner is the phrase "unprejudiced observation." He used this and similar terms roughly forty times in his major work, *The Philosophy of Freedom.*

The King James Bible uses a similar term: *behold.** It is derived from the Greek word *eido*—literally, "be sure to see." Christ stated, "Behold, I make all things new" (Rev. 21:5). *Behold* is often used in an epiphanic sense, to look past or through the physical to observe the spiritual. For instance, Raphael's Sistine Madonna depicts Mary holding the infant Jesus, but she is also presenting Him. She is both holding Him physically and presenting Him so that we might behold Him. Beholding the spiritual is a human capability that can be nourished. Mary is our prime example of heart knowledge and encourages us to behold Christ. After beholding a spiritual reality, we bear witness to its truth. Beholding and bearing witness are intimately connected. They are actually one. Joining beholding and bearing witness is a transformative, epistemological experience. "And ye shall know the truth, and the truth shall make you free" (John 8:32). If we behold Christ, we are bearing witness to Him. This leads to a Pauline experience. "Abide in Me, and I in you" (John 15:4).

Dr. Steiner called his work "spiritual science," which sounds at first like a contradiction, but on examination we find it to be a koan. How do we apply scientific thinking to spiritual phenomena? If we can use unprejudiced observation for external realities, why not also for internal and spiritual realities? If the test can be replicated by a scientist, it has validity. If it can be validated by other scientists, it has universality. We can affirm spiritual facts with the same scientific process in the "smithy" of our soul.**

---

*   See https://www.kingjamesbibleonline.org/behold/.

**   Joyce, *Portrait of the Artist as a Young Man*, p. 253.

When Christ was asked what are the two greatest commandments, His response is to love God with all your heart, soul, and mind. It is the definition of spiritual activity. This is a total commitment.

> Jesus said unto him, Thou shalt love the Lord thy God with all thy heart, and with all thy soul, and with all thy mind. This is the first and great commandment. And the second is like unto it, Thou shalt love thy neighbor as thyself. (Matt. 22:37–39)

Mary loved God with all her heart, soul, and mind. And she loved her neighbor as she did herself. We are forever indebted to Mary beholding Christ. Her love of Christ changed the world.

A Note on Translations

Translation is an art form. Translations from one language to another are always problematic. Idioms don't translate well. Word-for-word, literal translations miss the spirit of the ideas. The key is to express the idea, the image, which demands mastery of the spiritual experience and fluency in many languages.

I do not know Aramaic, Greek, Latin, or German. I am dependent on translations. My preferences are personal. I prefer the King James Bible in most quotations, even though it is archaic. It is the most poetic and presents the best images.

Dr. Steiner's ideas were expressed in his native German tongue. They are rich and complex. I prefer Marjorie Spock's translations because she heard Dr. Steiner speak, and when she translated his German into American English, she captured his images in a poetic manner.

Mary and The Immaculate Conception

This complex, controversial idea is not in the Bible and has been argued for centuries. The basic idea is that for Mary to have given birth to Christ, she had to be born without original sin—immaculate. St. Thomas Aquinas argued that if that were true, Mary would not need Christ's Resurrection, making Christ's salvific act unnecessary. Perhaps the idea is misconstrued. Maybe the idea is correct that for an individual to give birth to Christ within herself she must have an immaculate soul. If this thesis has merit, catharsis becomes a necessary process to cleanse oneself on the path to becoming immaculate. The Holy of Holies within us must be cleansed to be ready for the birth of Christ within us. Our inner altar has to be bare and immaculate. Mary is the best example of one who goes through catharsis to give birth to the Christ within.

Mary in the Bible

At the Crucifixion, the Turning Point of Time, there were only four of Christ's followers who stood with Christ throughout His Passion. They were His mother and her sister Mary, wife of Clopas; Mary Magdala; and the only man, John, the disciple whom Jesus loved. These brave souls endured the hideous torture and death via crucifixion of Mary's beloved son and their friend and teacher. We shudder when we contemplate this agony. For those brave souls who want to relive this moment, there are inspired works by stigmatics such as Anna Katherine Emmerich and Judith von Halle, who can bring you into this holy, sacred sacrifice.

Now there stood by the cross of Jesus his mother, and his mother's sister, Mary the wife of Cleophas, and Mary Magdalene.

When Jesus therefore saw his mother, and the disciple standing by, whom he loved, he saith unto his mother, Woman, behold thy son!

Then saith he to the disciple, Behold thy mother! And from that hour that disciple took her unto his own home.

After this, Jesus knowing that all things were now accomplished, that the scripture might be fulfilled, saith, I thirst.

Now there was set a vessel full of vinegar: and they filled a sponge with vinegar, and put it upon hyssop, and put it to his mouth.

When Jesus therefore had received the vinegar, he said, It is accomplished: and he bowed his head, and gave up the spirit. (John 19:25–30)

It is especially noteworthy that those courageous hearts were mainly women, not men. All the men, except John, had fled this horrendous scene. Mary, John, and the other women kept the vigil. They bore witness to the truth. Bearing witness is not the same as testifying at a trial. It is the birth of a new spiritual life, evidenced by the way in which the person thereafter leads one's life—i.e., a transformation. This term *bearing witness* is a key phrase for understanding the presence of Christ. The word *witness* is prominent in the beginning of St. John's Gospel and is used four times in the first eighteen verses. John's Gospel is dedicated to the twin mysteries of incarnation, "The word became flesh," and excarnation, "It is accomplished." Only by Christ incarnating and excarnating could the Resurrection occur. Bearing witness to the presence of Christ can occur only as a free act in the soul of each individual.

Dr. Steiner states that, at Christmas, the Feast of the Incarnation, we should look toward Easter, the Feast of Excarnation and Resurrection. Incarnation is the in-breath; excarnation is the out-breath. Each is connected intimately with the other. The joy we feel at Christmas is the birth of the Messiah. The joy we feel at Easter is the triumph of the spirit over death. We are all spiritually born anew. Death and life have been redeemed.

Mary, John, and the others became the first Christians by bearing witness to the truth of Christ's Crucifixion. This prepared them for the resurrected Christ. They were initiated through His death into His Resurrection, *"In Christo morimur; Per Spiritum Sanctum reviviscimus."* The English translation means "In Christ we die; through the Holy Spirit we are reborn." It is the ancient understanding of The Mystery of Golgotha.

His death and suffering were not a fiction. This act of divine love transformed these brave souls. They were born anew via this terrible catharsis. This catharsis was the birth pangs of their spiritual lives.

It is meaningful that Christ addressed his mother as "Woman." This was how God addressed Eve before the Fall. Eve was named Eve after the Fall. The designation of Mary as woman is directly connected with Eve. Mary is the second Eve and therefore the spiritual mother of us all.

Many in the ancient world conceived of the heart as the source of thinking. It was not only activity of the physical brain; there was also a deeper process that is intimately connected with the heart, as we read in this passage:

At Gibeon, Yahweh appeared to Solomon in a dream during the night. God said, "Ask what you would like me to give you." ...

Now, Yahweh my God, you have made your servant king in succession to David my father. But I am a very young man, unskilled in leadership.

And here is your servant, surrounded with your people whom you have chosen, a people so numerous that its number cannot be counted or reckoned.

So give your servant a heart to understand how to govern your people, how to discern between good and evil, for how could one otherwise govern such a great people as yours?

It pleased Yahweh that Solomon should have asked for this.

"Since you have asked for this," God said, "and not asked for long life for yourself or riches or the lives of your enemies but have asked for a discerning judgement for yourself, here and now I do what you ask. I give you a heart wise and shrewd as no one has had before and no one will have after you." (I Kings 3:5, 7–12)

Beholding the child, Simeon stated that Mary's child will be opposed by many and that she herself would suffer, that a sword would pierce her soul. All this will lead to thoughts of the heart, her innermost thoughts, being revealed.

And Simeon blessed them and said to Mary His mother, "Behold, this Child is appointed for the fall and rise of many in Israel, and for a sign to be opposed—and a sword will pierce even your own soul—to the end that thoughts from many hearts may be revealed." (Luke 2:34–35)

Some of the astounding last words from Christ were that Mary was to behold her son, John and that John was to behold his mother, Mary. From that moment John took Mary into his home. Legend has it that Mary lived with John for the rest of her life, even going to Ephesus to live with John. Creating this relationship is one of the most critical acts of Christ during His death throes. Its importance is essential to our understanding of Christ, Mary, John, Christianity, St. Michael, the Gospel of St. John, Anthroposophy, and *The Philosophy of Freedom.*

Let us take Christ at His word. His mother and his beloved friend are now mother and son. Their destiny and karma are intimately interconnected. The mother-son relationship is one of the most profound in all human experience. The one between Jesus and Mary was even more so. Steiner states in his *Fifth Gospel* that, as Jesus was going to encounter St. John for His baptism in the Jordan, He unburdened Himself to His beloved mother.

> His words did not merely go across to his mother, but they were like living beings that entered her heart. As the profound meaning of these words—a meaning full of suffering but also filled with profound love for humanity—entered her soul, she felt inwardly strengthened by a power that came from him, and she felt that her soul was changing.*

Throughout her life Mary had been prepared by Christ to have the strength to withstand His trial. Through this love of Christ, Mary's transformation began and was the first of many. After the Crucifixion, Mary gave birth to the Christ within her. She was one of the first Christians and, as such, the center of His followers (the church, which means a group, not a building or hierarchy). She experienced "Not I, but Christ liveth in me" (Gal. 2:20). Her soul, purified

---

* Steiner, *Isis Mary Sophia,* "The Fifth Gospel," p. 156.

by the Golgotha experience, was the virgin soul that gave birth to the Christ within her. Christ's followers called her mother.

This transformation of Mary was most evident to John, the apostle prepared by Christ on the most intimate level. Hence the phrase "the disciple whom Jesus loved" (John 21:7). This was the love that Christ bears for everyone. It was not singular; it was just that John had been prepared for it by his initiation into the spiritual realms as Lazarus. After his initiation, Lazarus was renamed John.

Christ had taught Mary and John and the rest of the disciples so that after the Resurrection they could spiritually see Him and bear witness to Christ's spirit of love. Without this spiritual concept of Christ, they would have been blind to the spiritual percept of Christ.

When John lived with Mary, he was in the presence of the most evolved of all human hearts—the one who courageously did what God willed, while also pondering it deep in her heart. This combination of heart and thinking is heartfelt knowledge, this is the Marian way. It lies behind all Christian thought and is best defined in the Gospel of St. John, in Anthroposophy, and especially in *The Philosophy of Freedom*. It is the key to the birth of the spirit. Marian knowledge is spiritual activity dedicated to the love of Christ and our sisters and brothers and hence all of humanity.

> He frees thoughts from their restriction to the head region and opens a way for them to the heart. He sets inner enthusiasm glowing, enabling man to give himself in soul devotion to everything that can be experienced in the light of thought. The Michael Age has arrived. Hearts are beginning to have thoughts. Enthusiasm is no longer

generated by obscure mysticism, but by inner clarity supported by thoughts.*

John wrote his Gospel from this Marian perspective. How could he do otherwise? Why else would Christ anoint them as mother and son? This Marian way to knowledge has many attributes. The central themes are the primacy of love and that the heart thinks. Other central themes, directly connected with the first two, are the humility and joy of standing in God's presence. Although this might appear contradictory, Mary is both humble and ecstatic! Her humility arose from deep experience of the divine grace and love of Christ, while her ecstasy is the result of finding her Messiah and her true nature—her spirit. She experienced the beatific vision of beholding the resurrected spiritual body of Christ while she was still in her physical body.

Birth (incarnation, or becoming) and death (excarnation, or passing away) are two realities that are certainties for all humans. These transitional moments are what we constantly prepare for and do. We are being born and dying all the time. Catharsis is how we purge what is unnecessary in order to give birth to new life. These birth and death pangs may be painful, but the joy afterward far outweighs the pain. Mary's way is the way of incarnation and affirmation. Mary has one word for following her spiritual intuitions—Yes! Where would we be without Mary's Yes?

By making the Father's will her will, Mary helped the Christ incarnate. Jesus taught us in the *Our Father* that we are co-creators with God by doing His will, "Thy Kingdom come, Thy will be done on earth as it is in heaven" (Matt. 6:10). Mary turned her will to incarnating God's will. She

---

*   Steiner, *The Michael Mystery*, pp. 3, 4.

was reifying God's will on earth as it is in heaven. By this
sacrificial way of life, she gave birth to the Divine Word, the
Christ, the Logos. Openness to the Lord and loving Him
and doing His will is a state of blessedness. "And Mary said,
Behold the handmaid of the Lord; be it unto me according
to thy word" (Luke 1:38).

We will consider the very few, though powerful, words
by and about Mary in the Gospels. The first statement about
Mary in Matthew is actually quite disturbing. This Gospel is
from Joseph's perspective, the descendant of David. Joseph,
being a just man, was considering a divorce after he discov-
ered his wife was pregnant before they were married.

> Now the birth of Jesus Christ was on this wise: When
> as his mother Mary was espoused to Joseph, before they
> came together, she was found with child of the Holy Spirit.
>
> Then Joseph her husband, being a just man, and not
> willing to make her a public example, was minded to put
> her away privily.
>
> But while he thought on these things, behold, the angel
> of the Lord appeared unto him in a dream, saying, Joseph,
> thou son of David, fear not to take unto thee Mary thy
> wife: for that which is conceived in her is of the Holy Spirit.
>
> And she shall bring forth a son, and thou shalt call his
> name Jesus: for he shall save his people from their sins.
>
> Now all this was done, that it might be fulfilled which
> was spoken of the Lord by the prophet, saying,
>
> Behold, a virgin shall be with child, and shall bring
> forth a son, and they shall call his name Emmanuel, which
> being interpreted is, God with us.
>
> Then Joseph being raised from sleep did as the angel
> of the Lord had bidden him, and took unto him his wife:
>
> And knew her not till she had brought forth her first-
> born son: and he called his name Jesus. (Matt. 1:18–26)

Joseph had an epiphany and he listened to the angel who foretold the birth of Emmanuel, God with us. Remember, Mary could have been stoned to death for being pregnant before her marriage to Joseph. Clearly, Joseph was a righteous man who acted in accordance with his spiritual insight. Steiner might call this moral imagination. Matthew's Gospel does not include a word from Mary. Nevertheless, she was a vessel of the Holy Spirit, and Joseph was the key. It is important to note that Mary had a special relationship with the Holy Spirit, one that would be pronounced at Pentecost, in which she was often depicted as the center of the group, and even as the person through whom the Holy Spirit entered the group.

In Mark there was no nativity and, like Matthew, John the Baptist was of great importance in the beginning—even more so than Mary. The word *mother* was used a few times to note that Mary was present, but she was not portrayed as speaking or acting directly. She was in the background, like water in a painting. She was present but left few footprints.

In Luke, John the Baptist was again described as the foretold prophet of the Messiah. The angel was explicit when saying that, as Malachi had predicted in the last book of the Old Testament, Elijah would return to announce the coming of the Messiah.

> Behold, I will send you Elijah the prophet before the coming of the great and dreadful day of the LORD:
>
> And he shall turn the heart of the fathers to the children, and the heart of the children to their fathers, lest I come and smite the earth with a curse. (Mal. 4:5–6)

Luke's angel stated to Zacharias that John the Baptist is Elijah.

And there appeared unto him an angel of the Lord standing on the right side of the altar of incense.

And when Zacharias saw him, he was troubled, and fear fell upon him.

But the angel said unto him, Fear not, Zacharias: for thy prayer is heard; and thy wife Elisabeth shall bear thee a son, and thou shalt call his name John.

And thou shalt have joy and gladness; and many shall rejoice at his birth.

For he shall be great in the sight of the Lord, and shall drink neither wine nor strong drink; and he shall be filled with the Holy Spirit, even from his mother's womb.

And many of the children of Israel shall he turn to the Lord their God.

And he shall go before him in the spirit and power of Elijah, to turn the hearts of the fathers to the children, and the disobedient to the wisdom of the just; to make ready a people prepared for the Lord. (Luke 1:11–17)

Christ made it clear to His disciples that John is Elijah.

For all the prophets and the law prophesied until John.

And if you are willing to receive it, he is Elijah who is to come.

He who has ears to hear, let him hear! (Matt. 11:13–15)

Christ again declared John as Elijah later in Matthew.

And his disciples asked him, saying, Why then say the scribes that Elijah must first come?

And Jesus answered and said unto them, Elijah truly shall first come, and restore all things.

But I say unto you, That Elijah is come already, and they knew him not, but have done unto him whatsoever they listed. Likewise, shall also the Son of man suffer of them.

Then the disciples understood that he spake unto them of John the Baptist. (Matt. 17:10–13)

In Luke, Mary becomes evident and has a beatific presence befitting the Mother of the Messiah. The Annunciation is one of the most beautiful moments in the Bible. It is also known as the Feast of the Incarnation (*Festum Incarnationis*) and *Conceptio Christi* (Christ's Conception). *The Annunciation* (1436) by Fra Angelico is a stunning work of devotion and art. The Prado version is in Madrid. The colors are still vibrant after nearly 600 years. Mary's gown with its majestic blue shimmers in all its glory. The folds in the angel's gown are creased and exact with a light blue undergarment.

There are Adam and Eve leaving the garden. Eve was seduced by Lucifer. In contrast, Gabriel approached Mary with awe and reverence. Mary, the new Eve, was filled with humility. Not even God could force Mary's free decision. Mary, out of her heartfelt love of God, agreed to God's will. Mary received the Lord's will that the Logos should become flesh. Her yes is one of the defining acts of human freedom. Her yes allowed Jesus to incarnate and redeem all.

The Trinity is evident in the picture from the hands of God in the upper left to the Holy Spirit as a dove flying to Mary's heart and Christ above the column.

The Annunciation *(c. 1430) by Fra Angelico*
(Prado, Madrid)

This painting is the story of the Fall and its answer, the Incarnation of the Logos, all in one. It comes through a young woman who will crush the head of Satan. Dr. Steiner has a verse that seems appropriate for this scene.

> From the luminous heights of the Spirit,
> May God's clear light ray forth
> Into those human souls
> Who are intent on seeking
> The grace of the Spirit,
> The light of the Spirit,
> The life of the Spirit.
>
> May He live
> In the hearts
> In the inmost souls
> Of those of us

Who feel ourselves gathered
together here
In His name.*

Denise Levertov captured the solemnity of this moment in her poem.

ANNUNCIATION

"Hail, space for the uncontained God"
From the Agathistos Hymn,
Greece, VIc

We know the scene: the room, variously furnished,
almost always a lectern, a book; always
the tall lily.
        Arrived on solemn grandeur of great wings,
the angelic ambassador, standing or hovering,
whom she acknowledges, a guest.

But we are told of meek obedience. No one mentions
courage.
        The engendering Spirit
did not enter her without consent.
        God waited.

She was free
to accept or to refuse, choice
integral to humanness.

———————————————

Aren't there annunciations
of one sort or another
in most lives?
        Some unwillingly

---

*   Steiner, *Verses and Meditations*, p. 195. Given by Rudolf Steiner in 1913 to the leader of the Emerson group in London, Mrs. Cull, for use by that group.

undertake great destinies,
enact them in sullen pride,
uncomprehending.
    More often
those moments
    when roads of light and storm
    open from darkness in a man or woman,
are turned away from

in dread, in a wave of weakness, in despair
and with relief.
Ordinary lives continue.
                God does not smite them.
But the gates close, the pathway vanishes.

She had been a child who played, ate, slept
like any other child–but unlike others,
wept only for pity, laughed
in joy not triumph.
Compassion and intelligence
fused in her, indivisible.

Called to a destiny more momentous
than any in all of Time,
she did not quail,
    only asked
a simple, "How can this be?"
and gravely, courteously,
took to heart the angel's reply,
the astounding ministry she was offered:

to bear in her womb
Infinite weight and lightness; to carry
in hidden, finite inwardness,
nine months of Eternity; to contain
in slender vase of being,

the sum of power–
in narrow flesh,
the sum of light.
        Then bring to birth,
push out into air, a Man-child
needing, like any other,
milk and love—

but who was God.

This was the moment no one speaks of,
when she could still refuse.

A breath unbreathed,
        Spirit,

            suspended,

                waiting.

She did not cry, "I cannot. I am not worthy,"
Nor, "I have not the strength."
She did not submit with gritted teeth,
            raging, coerced.
Bravest of all humans,
         consent illumined her.
The room filled with its light,
the lily glowed in it,
        and the iridescent wings.
Consent,
        courage unparalleled,
opened her utterly.*

---

*   "Annunciation" by Denise Levertov, from *A Door in the Hive*, copyright ©1989 by Denise Levertov. Reprinted by permission of New Directions Publishing Corp.

Levertov's lines illumine the wonder of Mary and emphasize the courage of a young woman who changed the world with her free consent.

> But we are told of meek obedience. No one mentions courage.
> The engendering Spirit
> did not enter her without consent.
> God waited.

…and:

> Consent,
> courage unparalleled,
> opened her utterly.

The miracle of the Annunciation would make any human quake in the face of an encounter with Gabriel, but Mary maintained her equilibrium.

> And in the sixth month the angel Gabriel was sent from God unto a city of Galilee, named Nazareth,
> To a virgin espoused to a man whose name was Joseph, of the house of David; and the virgin's name was Mary.
> And the angel came in unto her, and said, Hail, thou that art highly favored, the Lord is with thee: blessed art thou among women.
> And when she saw him, she was troubled at his saying, and cast in her mind what manner of salutation this should be. (Luke 1:26–29)

Can you imagine being in the presence of an angel and then being majestically greeted with such profound language? Gabriel's words became immortalized as part of the Hail Mary prayer in a slightly different translation, "Hail Mary, full of grace, the Lord is with thee: blessed art thou among women." Humble Mary could not understand the greeting by the angel. She cast in her mind, what a wonderful image of fishing for an answer!

> And the angel said unto her, Fear not, Mary: for thou hast found favor with God.
>
> And, behold, thou shalt conceive in thy womb, and bring forth a son, and shalt call his name JESUS.
>
> He shall be great, and shall be called the Son of the Highest: and the Lord God shall give unto him the throne of his father David:
>
> And he shall reign over the house of Jacob forever; and of his kingdom there shall be no end.
>
> Then said Mary unto the angel, How shall this be, seeing I know not a man? (Luke 1:30–34)

Courageous, practical Mary asked how can that be since I have never known a man? Even in the presence of an angel, she did not succumb to fear.

> And the angel answered and said unto her, The Holy Spirit shall come upon thee, and the power of the Highest shall overshadow thee: therefore, also that holy thing which shall be born of thee shall be called the Son of God.
>
> And, behold, thy cousin Elisabeth, she hath also conceived a son in her old age: and this is the sixth month with her, who was called barren. (Luke 1:35–36)

The angel Gabriel gave the definitive definition of God.

> For with God nothing shall be impossible. (Luke 1:37)

And Mary responded with the ultimate Yes to do God's will. The sublime act of freedom, "Be it unto me according to thy word." Note Mary's use of the term *word*. The Logos literally becomes flesh.

> And Mary said, Behold the handmaid of the Lord; be it unto me according to thy word. And the angel departed from her. (Luke 1:38)

Mary's response was not a singular act occurring only once. She constantly did God's will. She said yes, every day, all the way to the Passion and Golgotha. All the way to *The Pietà*. Did Mary know that her aged, barren cousin was pregnant? Remember Elizabeth was distant. Mary traveled from Nazareth to Ein Kerem, roughly eighty miles in a straight line, but more over the hilly paths. Mary arose and went in haste to Elizabeth to affirm what she had been told by the angel.

> And Mary arose in those days, and went into the hill country with haste, into a city of Judah. (Luke 1:39)

John leaped in Elizabeth's womb in recognition of Mary and the Jesus child she had inside her womb. He knew. Ever the forerunner, this was the reason John was born—to proclaim the presence of Jesus. John bears witness before he is born! John beheld Jesus in Mary.

> And entered into the house of Zacharias, and saluted Elisabeth.
>
> And it came to pass, that, when Elisabeth heard the salutation of Mary, the babe leaped in her womb; and Elisabeth was filled with the Holy Spirit:
>
> And she spake out with a loud voice, and said, Blessed art thou among women, and blessed is the fruit of thy womb.
>
> And whence is this to me, that the mother of my Lord should come to me?
>
> For, lo, as soon as the voice of thy salutation sounded in mine ears, the babe leaped in my womb for joy.

And blessed is she that believed: for there shall be a performance of those things which were told her from the Lord. (Luke 1:40–45)

The angel was correct. Elizabeth was pregnant. Mary knew that he was also telling the truth about her and the miraculous birth of Jesus. Elizabeth was filled with the Holy Spirit and initiated the reverent mood of awe concerning the advent of the Messiah. Elizabeth's speech then repeated the phrase from Gabriel's speech and gave another part of the Hail Mary prayer, "Blessed art thou among women, and blessed is the fruit of thy womb." Mary became inspired. In divine rapture she sang praises to God for the birth of the Messiah, His divine son. All the prophecies of God's covenant with His chosen people were about to be fulfilled.

And Mary said, My soul doth magnify the Lord,
    And my spirit hath rejoiced in God my Savior.
    For he hath regarded the low estate of his hand-
maiden: for, behold, from henceforth all generations
shall call me blessed.
    For he that is mighty hath done to me great things;
and holy is his name.
    And his mercy is on them that fear him from genera-
tion to generation.
    He hath shewed strength with his arm; he hath
scattered the proud in the imagination of their hearts.
    He hath put down the mighty from their seats and
exalted them of low degree.
    He hath filled the hungry with good things; and the
rich he hath sent empty away.
    He hath helped his servant Israel, in remembrance
of his mercy;
    As he spake to our fathers, to Abraham, and to his
seed for ever. (Luke 1:46–55)

The Magnificat, which means magnify, also has a distinct connection with the Beatitudes. Consider the cathartic statement by Christ: "Blessed are the pure of heart, for they shall see God." One could consider Mary as a living example of the virtues embodied in the Beatitudes and, therefore, she was with God. *Beatitude* means happy. A more literal translation into contemporary English may be "possessing an inward contentedness and joy that is not affected by the physical circumstances" (Wikipedia).

By bearing witness or beholding the presence of Christ, Mary's soul magnified the grace God had shone upon her. She reflected His presence as the moon reflects the sun. She glowed with His presence and grace!

Let us look at some of the beatitudes through the prism of Mary. Jesus may have been using His mother as a proof of His statements.

> Blessed are the poor in spirit, for theirs is the kingdom of heaven. (Matt. 5:3)

If by poor in spirit, we mean someone who begs for God, then Mary and Israel would be extreme examples of spiritual poverty. She knows that she is incomplete. Mary stated that she is in a low estate—i.e., she and all of Israel have been begging for redemption for hundreds of years. They are poor in spirit. "For he hath regarded the low estate of his handmaiden."

> Blessed are those who mourn, for they will be comforted. (Matt. 5:4)

Who mourns more than Mary? She watched her son get whipped, be spit upon, carry a cross, be crucified, and then die? Who could live through that torture? But she will be comforted by the resurrected Christ.

> Blessed are the meek, for they will inherit the earth.
>
> (Matt. 5:5)

Again, who is more meek than Mary, the mother of the Messiah? Who, in the words of Paul, is patient, kind, and not jealous and bears all things and endures all things?

> Love is patient,
> love is kind and is not jealous;
> love does not brag and is not arrogant,
> does not act unbecomingly; it does not seek its own,
> is not provoked,
> does not take into account a wrong suffered,
> does not rejoice in unrighteousness,
> but rejoices with the truth;
> bears all things, believes all things, hopes all things,
> endures all things.
> Love never fails. (1 Cor. 13:4–8)

Mary was a righteous person. She lived to do the Lord's will. That is the definition of righteous.

> Blessed are those who hunger and thirst for righteousness,
> for they will be filled. (Matt. 5:6)

Mary's mercy extends to all. She is kind from the wedding feast guests to the children of Lourdes and Fatima.

> Blessed are the merciful, for they will be shown mercy.
>
> (Matt. 5:7)

This may be the clearest example of Mary as the shining example of the Beatitudes. Because of the purity of her heart, she could bear Christ.

Blessed are the pure in heart, for they will see God.

(Matt. 5:8)

But that union with God has a price, catharsis. We have to purify ourselves. Dr. Steiner stated the very difficult truth.

All knowledge that can truly be called great is born from pain, from inner travail. When through the means for the attainment of knowledge described in anthroposophic spiritual science one tries to tread the path into the higher worlds, the goal can be reached only by experiencing pain. Without having suffered, suffered intensely, and thereby having become free from the oppression of pain, no one can come to know the spiritual world.*

Polyptych of the Misericordia (1445–1462), by Piero della Francesca (Museo Civico di Pinacoteca Comunale, Tuscany, Italy)

---

* Steiner, *The Festivals and their Meaning*, p. 284.

Mary was warned not only by Simeon that a sword will pierce her heart, but also by Gabriel in the Annunciation. It was shown by some artists that Mary had been given insight by Gabriel regarding the Crucifixion. In the *Polyptych of the Misericordia* by Piero della Francesca, Gabriel stands to the left of Mary at the Crucifixion. Mary's Yes takes on even more solemnity. She said Yes all the way to Golgotha. Her entire life was a Yes.

THE GOSPEL OF ST. JOHN

Let us examine the Gospel of St. John from this Marian perspective. First is the explicit reference to the majestic beginning of Genesis in the Old Testament. From Genesis, we read of the beauty of God's creation and the centrality of Light. Please note that God *spoke* Light into existence. The Word of God creates.

> In the beginning, God created the heavens and the earth. The earth was without form and void, and darkness was over the face of the deep. And the Spirit of God was hovering over the face of the waters.
> And God said, "Let there be light," and there was light. And God saw that the light was good. And God separated the light from the darkness. God called the light Day, and the darkness he called Night. And there was evening and there was morning, the first day. (Gen. 1:1–5)

John's Gospel begins with a term or idea that was central to the Ephesian Mystery center. John's epiphanic understanding was that the Logos is the prime mover, the agent or creator of creation. Before there was anything, the Spirit had to create creativity. John realized the Greeks were describing Christ, the Logos, the Alpha and the Omega. The being or Spirit that created creativity was Christ, the Logos. John's Genesis version therefore predates the story of Genesis in the Old Testament! It happened before Genesis, for without the Logos or Christ there was nothing that was made.

This cosmic vision is about Christ, the agent or source of creativity. This predates time and the birth of the universe. It is the definition of Incarnation. It is the pouring of the spiritual into the physical. Christ is the source of life and light. These terms represent not only physical life and light, but also spiritual life and light. Light is intimately connected with creation. God's first words created light and separated it from darkness. In John's Gospel, light is again immanent and a manifestation of life and a triumphant Christ. The darkness cannot overcome it.

> In the beginning was the Logos, and the Logos was with God, and the Logos was God. He was in the beginning with God. All things were made through him, and without him was not any thing made that was made. In him was life, and the life was the light of men. The light shines in the darkness, and the darkness has not overcome it. (John 1:1–5)

There is then the beautiful description of John the Baptist, the forerunner of the Christ as predicted in Malachi, the last book of the Old Testament. Malachi predicted that Elijah must come first. Christ stated that John was Elijah. One of the critical acts of John was to bear witness to Christ. This is not to bear witness in a legal sense, but is more encompassing. It means that, after encountering the Christ, a person will thereafter be transformed. History has changed; the Messiah has arrived. In this beautiful rendition of Christ's incarnation, John's mission was to bear witness to the light, the Messiah. Bearing witness is a birth process. It is Marian in nature. It is the definition of a mother, giving birth.

> There was a man sent from God, whose name was John. He came as a witness, to bear witness about the light, that

all might believe through him. He was not the light, but came to bear witness about the light. (John 1:6–8)

The Marian birth theme continues in the next stanzas. The world was made through Him. The act of reception is similar to the act of conception. The womb receives the child. There is an emptiness or stillness that is necessary for creation. From this stillness and emptiness, conception can occur, but only if there is a free act of receiving. Christ is pouring himself into incarnation. Emmanuel or God with us is present. Do we use our freedom to receive Him?

> The true light, which enlightens everyone, was coming into the world. He was in the world, and the world was made through him, yet the world did not know him. He came to his own, and his own people did not receive him. But to all who did receive him, who believed in his name, he gave the right to become children of God, who were born, not of blood nor of the will of the flesh nor of the will of man, but of God. (John 1:9–13)

Through our relationship with Christ, we are given the right to become children of God, *Ex Deo nascimur,* Through God we are born. We are spiritual beings. We are loved and are spirit as well as flesh. This gift of being born of God is the most precious gift of all time.

> And the Word became flesh and dwelt among us, and we have seen his glory, glory as of the only Son from the Father, full of grace and truth. John bore witness about him, and cried out, "This was he of whom I said, He who comes after me ranks before me, because he was before me." And from his fullness we have all received, grace upon grace. For the law was given through Moses; grace and truth came through Jesus Christ. No one has ever seen

God; the only begotten Son, who is at the Father's side, he has made him known. (John 1:14–18)

The incarnation of the infinite into the finite, the Logos into the flesh occurred so that the flesh may have the grace to become the Logos. *Glory,* to the early Christians, meant the presence of God. John the Evangelist was stating that Christians have perceived Christ's glory, His resurrection. John the Baptist also bore witness and affirmed that Christ is the Messiah, the anointed one. Christ, from his fullness, continues to pour grace upon us. Do we through our transformations bear witness?

Mary, in the very beginning of John's Gospel at the wedding of Cana, understood the embarrassment of the hosts running out of wine. Ever practical, Mary asked her son to help. As at the cross, Jesus refers to her as woman as God did with Eve.

> And the third day there was a marriage in Cana of Galilee; and the mother of Jesus was there:
> And both Jesus was called, and his disciples, to the marriage. And when they wanted wine, the mother of Jesus saith unto him, They have no wine. Jesus saith unto her, Woman, what have I to do with thee? mine hour is not yet come. His mother saith unto the servants, Whatsoever he saith unto you, do it. (John 2:2–5)

Mary gave the definitive proclamation to followers of Christ. "Whatever he saith unto you, do it." Jesus then performed His first public miracle and changed water into wine, as He will perform at the act of Transubstantiation at the Last Supper and down thought the ages in the ritual act of communion. All started by Mary's request.

A central theme in Platonic philosophy is Socrates' statement defining himself as "a midwife to ideas." Socrates assisted others in the birthing, or incarnation, of ideas. Socrates did not create the ideas; he helped in the delivery. For Dr. Steiner, ideas are alive in the spirit. These ideas are beyond intellectual concepts; they are spiritual realities. There is a vitality to true, spiritual thinking that is alive and vibrant. The act of spiritual thinking is a spiritual activity. A spiritually active person affirms his or her spiritual nature through this activity. The individual is born again through sacramental thinking. The Logos is the reality of the incarnating Christ. All Christian thought is centered on being "born again," or born in the spirit.

> Jesus answered and said unto him, Verily, verily, I say unto thee, Except a man be born again, he cannot see the kingdom of God.
>
> Nicodemus saith unto him, How can a man be born when he is old? can he enter the second time into his mother's womb, and be born?
>
> Jesus answered, Verily, verily, I say unto thee, Except a man be born of water and of the Spirit, he cannot enter into the kingdom of God. That which is born of the flesh is flesh; and that which is born of the Spirit is spirit. Marvel not that I said unto thee, Ye must be born again. The wind bloweth where it listeth, and thou hearest the sound thereof, but canst not tell whence it cometh, and whither it goeth: so is every one that is born of the Spirit. (John 3:3–8)

Mary almost disappeared from the rest of the Gospels. There are no words concerning her meeting the risen Christ. The absence of a written meeting does not prove that she did not meet with Him after the Resurrection. She was clearly present in *The Act of the Apostles.*

> They all joined together constantly in prayer, along with the women and Mary the mother of Jesus, and with his brothers. (Acts 1:14)

Mary was often depicted by artists in the center of the Apostles when the Holy Spirit descended upon them just as Gabriel proclaimed in The Annunciation. "The Holy Spirit will come upon you and the power of the Most High will overshadow you" (Luke 1:35). In the following picture, she was not only the center of the action, she was also directly below the Holy Spirit.

Pentecost (Jan Joest van Kalkar, 1505–1508)

Mary in the The Book of Revelation

The most difficult book in the bible has a frightening and beautiful vision of Mary. She is clothed with the sun and adorned with twelve stars. Mary is central in the battle with the serpent. The serpent makes war with her seed—those who keep the commandments and follow the testimony of Jesus Christ.

A statue of Mary in Strasbourg Cathedral (1859)

And there appeared a great wonder in heaven; a woman clothed with the sun, and the moon under her feet, and upon her head a crown of twelve stars: And she being with child cried, travailing in birth, and pained to be delivered.

And there appeared another wonder in heaven; and behold a great red dragon, having seven heads and ten horns, and seven crowns upon his heads. And his tail drew the third part of the stars of heaven, and did cast them to the earth: and the dragon stood before the woman which was ready to be delivered, for to devour her child as soon as it was born. And she brought forth a man child, who was to rule all nations with a rod of iron: and her child was caught up unto God, and to his throne. And the woman fled into the wilderness, where she hath a place prepared of God, that they should feed her there a thousand two hundred and threescore days.

And there was war in heaven: Michael and his angels fought against the dragon; and the dragon fought and his angels, and prevailed not; neither was their place found any more in heaven. And the great dragon was cast out, that old serpent, called the Devil, and Satan, which deceiveth the whole world: he was cast out into the earth, and his angels were cast out with him.

And I heard a loud voice saying in heaven, Now is come salvation, and strength, and the kingdom of our God, and the power of his Christ: for the accuser of our brethren is cast down, which accused them before our God day and night. And they overcame him by the blood of the Lamb, and by the word of their testimony; and they loved not their lives unto the death. Therefore rejoice, ye heavens, and ye that dwell in them. Woe to the inhabiters of the earth and of the sea! For the devil is come down unto you, having great wrath, because he knoweth that he hath but a short time.

And when the dragon saw that he was cast unto the earth, he persecuted the woman which brought forth the man child. And to the woman were given two wings of a great eagle, that she might fly into the wilderness, into her place, where she is nourished for a time, and times, and half a time, from the face of the serpent. And the serpent cast out of his mouth water as a flood after the woman, that he might cause her to be carried away of the flood. And the earth helped the woman, and the earth opened her mouth, and swallowed up the flood which the dragon cast out of his mouth.

And the dragon was wroth with the woman and went to make war with the remnant of her seed, which keep the commandments of God, and have the testimony of Jesus Christ. (Rev. 12:1–17)

These words depict the epic, horrific battle between the dragon and Mary and her seed, a battle that continues to the present day and into the future. Mary gives birth in the midst of this great battle with the Dragon. Her goal is to do the will of God, "And she brought forth a man child, who was to rule all nations with a rod of iron: and her child was caught up unto God, and to his throne" (Rev. 12:5).

While these words may be the last words on Mary in the Bible, they are not the last words on Mary. Mary has appeared again and again throughout time. She continues to say Yes.

THE PHILOSOPHY OF FREEDOM

Let us now consider *The Philosophy of Freedom* in this Marian light. In Dr. Steiner's lecture "The Nature of The Virgin Sophia and of The Holy Spirit," which is the last lecture in *the Gospel of St. John*, Steiner unites all these themes. Dr. Steiner states that *The Philosophy of Freedom* can be a cathartic experience if one inwardly experiences and lives into the ideas in the book. Dr. Steiner stated in the aforementioned lecture that, through the cathartic experience, the virgin Sophia (soul) becomes the purified astral body and can encounter the Holy Spirit, which gives birth to the Christ within. Dr. Steiner then explicitly states that the Gospel of St. John is the record of that catharsis of the soul, and that by living into that Gospel one can experience Christian initiation. He went as far as to state in this lecture that daily reading of the first eighteen verses of St. John's Gospel can transform your soul. The Christ forces within the verses can lead the meditating person to initiation with Christ. Thus, the Christ, the Logos, becomes flesh within us.

It is easy to regard *The Philosophy of Freedom* as an intellectual tract of Germanic logic. This is a serious disservice. Given the preceding considerations of the Marian way, consider the following quotation from *The Philosophy of Freedom*: "A truth that comes to us from outside always bears the stamp of uncertainty. We can believe only what appears to each one of us in our own hearts as truth."*

Since Dr. Steiner viewed intuitive thinking as a spiritual experience, he saw it as luminous; thinking has the ability to become a spiritual organ. Therefore, we can experience the Marian question with a different wording: "How can this be, since I have not experienced this creative aspect of thinking?" The answer comes back, "With God all things are possible" (Matt. 19:26). God has created thinking so that thinking can give us the spiritual experience to help resurrect our thinking. Spiritual thinking activates our spiritual nature. This spiritual nature bears witness to its own existence via this thinking. It becomes a self-affirming realization. I can think spiritually, therefore I am a spiritual being. This is the ultimate proof statement—direct experience of the spiritual through sense-free thinking! We can behold ourselves as spiritual beings when we are engaged in spiritual activity. This internal epiphany that we are spiritual beings in a spiritual world is the definition of freedom. Christ's truth has freed us from the illusions and limitations of sense-bound thinking.

This is the modern birth of the Logos. Mary and John are the midwives to our spirit, the Christ within each of us. Through heartfelt thinking dedicated to and filled with love, we can give birth to our Christ nature, our true Omega.

> Thinking all too readily leaves us cold in recollection; it is as if the life of the soul had dried out. Yet this is really nothing but the strongly marked shadow of its real nature—warm, luminous, and penetrating deeply into the phenomena of the world. This penetration is brought about by a power flowing through the activity of thinking

* Steiner, *The Philosophy of Freedom*, p. xxvii.

itself—the power of love in its spiritual form. There are no grounds here for the objection that to discern love in the activity of thinking is to project into thinking a feeling, namely, love. For in truth this objection is but a confirmation of what we have been saying. If we turn toward thinking *in its essence*, we find in it both feeling and will, and these in the depths of their reality; if we turn away from thinking toward "mere" feeling and will, we lose from these their true reality.*

Let us think of Mary's virgin soul as a womb or as an altar that was clean and spare. It awaited. It was receptive. Mary receded, so that Christ may incarnate. This humble yet courageous receptivity is the paradigm for spiritual thinking or spiritual activity. This is why Steiner emphasizes that for every spiritual step, one should take three moral steps. We must cleanse ourselves before we enter the holy of holies. Otherwise, we defile the spirit and can cause immense difficulties. We should rejoice at the necessity of catharsis and sacrifice to enter the spiritual. God is protecting us from our lower selves. Mary is our example. She prepared her soul for the manifestation of Christ, Emmanuel, God with us.

> Once we appreciate this, we can no longer fail to notice what a peculiar kind of relationship there is between the human organization and the thinking itself. For this organization contributes nothing to the essential nature of thinking but recedes whenever the activity of thinking makes its appearance; it suspends its own activity, it yields ground; and on the ground thus left empty, the thinking appears. The essence which is active in thinking has a twofold function: first, it represses the activity of the human organization; secondly, it steps into its place. For even the former, the repression of the physical organization, is a

---

*   Ibid., pp. 119–20.

consequence of the activity of thinking, and more particularly of that part of this activity which prepares the *manifestation* of thinking. *

The central image of Mary is her unending love for Christ. This love freed her from the false gods of egotism and materialism and transformed her spirit. She followed Christ out of pure love for Him. This is the definition of a free act.

> While I am performing the action I am influenced by a moral maxim insofar as it can live in me intuitively; it is bound up with my *love* for the objective that I want to realize through my action. I ask no man and no rule, "Shall I perform this action?"—but carry it out as soon as I have grasped the idea of it. This alone makes it *my* action. If a man acts only because he accepts certain moral standards, his action is the outcome of the principles that compose his moral code. He merely carries out orders. He is a superior automaton. Inject some stimulus to action into his mind, and at once the clockwork of his moral principles will set itself in motion and run its prescribed course, so as to result in an action that is Christian, or humane, or seemingly unselfish, or calculated to promote the progress of civilization. Only when I follow my love for my objective is it I myself who act. I act, at this level of morality, not because I acknowledge a lord over me, or an external authority, or a so-called inner voice; I acknowledge no external principle for my action, because I have found in myself the ground for my action—namely, my love of the action. I do not work out mentally whether my action is good or bad; I carry it out because I *love* it.**

---

*   Ibid., p. 123.

**   Ibid., pp. 135–36.

This quotation defines the relationship between Jesus and Mary, illustrating that their love-filled relationship is a paradigm for all other relationships. This conversation between Jesus and Mary occurred just before Jesus went to His Baptism by John in the Jordan. Their relationship is the definition of communion and is available to all. Each person can experience the loved one in her heart.

> His words did not merely go across to his mother, but they were like living beings that entered her heart. As the profound meaning of these words—a meaning full of suffering but also filled with profound love for humanity—entered her soul, she felt inwardly strengthened by a power that came from him, and she felt that her soul was changing.*

The following is a long quotation, but compare it with the words just quoted from the book *Isis Mary Sophia*. Similar themes are "Living beings that entered her heart" and "experiencing the content of another's consciousness," illustrating the potential of humans for intimate soul experiences.

From the appendix in *The Philosophy of Freedom*:

> Added to the new edition, 1918:
> What is it, in the first instance, that I have before me when I confront another person? The most immediate thing is the bodily appearance of the other person as given to me in sense perception; then, perhaps, the auditory perception of what he is saying, and so on. I do not merely stare at all this, but it sets my thinking activity in motion. Through the thinking with which I confront the other person, the percept of him becomes, as it were, transparent to the mind. I am bound to admit that when I grasp the percept with my thinking, it is not at all the

---

* Steiner, *Isis Mary Sophia,* "The Fifth Gospel," p. 156.

same thing as appeared to the outer senses. In what is a direct appearance to the senses, something else is indirectly revealed. The mere sense appearance extinguishes itself at the same time as it confronts me. But what it reveals through this extinguishing compels me as a thinking being to extinguish my own thinking as long as I am under its influence, and to put *its* thinking in the place of mine. I then grasp *its* thinking in my thinking as an experience like my own. I have really perceived another person's thinking. The immediate percept, extinguishing itself as sense appearance, is grasped by my thinking, and this is a process lying wholly within my consciousness and consisting in this, that the other person's thinking takes the place of mine. Through the self-extinction of the sense appearance, the separation between the two spheres of consciousness is actually overcome. This expresses itself in my consciousness through the fact that while experiencing the content of another person's consciousness I experience my own consciousness as little as I experience it in dreamless sleep. Just as in dreamless sleep my waking consciousness is eliminated, so in my perceiving of the content of another person's consciousness the content of my own is eliminated. The illusion that it is not so only comes about because in perceiving the other person, firstly, the extinction of the content of one's own consciousness gives place not to unconsciousness, as it does in sleep, but to the content of the other person's consciousness, and secondly, the alternations between extinguishing and lighting up again of my own self-consciousness follow too rapidly to be generally noticed.*

A central insight by Dr. Steiner is that the spiritual world is not some amorphous sea of non-differentiated spirit. There are distinct spiritual beings with strong proclivities and abilities. There are positive beings engaged in humanity's

* Steiner, *The Philosophy of Freedom*, pp. 224–26.

evolution and negative beings who thwart humanity's progression. Dr. Steiner and many others have experienced these beings and are capable of naming them. It is important to understand that these beings are individuals, just as we are, and have specific tasks. Christ is aided by Mary, St. John, St. Michael and countless other angelic beings to help us. By following the Marian path, we can encounter them and have communion with Christ. We should rejoice!

From Annunciation to Pentecost and beyond, Mary is open to the Holy Spirit. As Christ stated, "Blessed rather are those who hear the word of God and keep it" (Luke 11:28). This internal hearing and acting from that intuition, bearing witness, is the goal of *The Philosophy of Freedom*, a Marian work. Dr. Steiner stated a modern Magnificat, a modern bearing witness. "Hence every man, in his thinking, lays hold of the universal primordial Being which pervades all men. To live in reality, filled with the content of thought, is at the same time to live in God."*

Why was Dr. Steiner so concerned with thinking? Because we live in the age of the consciousness (or spiritual) soul. The goal of this age is to bring the instinctive into the full clarity of consciousness. We have proceeded from The Age of Faith to The Age of Knowledge. One of the most dramatic statements at the beginning of our age is Descartes' famous *Cogito ergo sum*, I think therefore I am. Descartes lived in an age of skepticism, when all knowledge was questioned, even the validity of thought and logic. He searched for an Archimedean principle that could be used as a lever to combat nihilistic skepticism. In his pondering, he took the skeptics position and imagined an Evil Genius. This being had an infinite capacity to deceive humanity. Think

* Ibid., p. 215.

of the Orwellian Big Brother as God! Dr. Steiner chose the names *Ahriman* and *Lucifer* for the negative beings.

Life was considered an illusion that could not be understood. The East calls it *maya*. Descartes realized that, even if such skepticism were valid, it does not negate existence. In fact, doubt proves existence. If I am doubting, I am thinking. Each person can doubt and think, even in a world of illusions. To Descartes the mathematician, this was the equation he was searching for. Thinking is proof of existence; if you think, you must exist. QED, *Cogito ergo sum*. Thinking = Existence. Of course, there is endless debate over this statement and how one might use logic and what *therefore* means. But it is a classic statement of proof of the inherent, self-affirming clarity of thinking. Thinking has a present tense and immediacy that is central to a human being. Thinking persists. Our very consciousness of self demands thinking. Without thinking we could not realize ourselves as distinct individuals.

Dr. Steiner took Descartes' statement in an evolutionary sense and proposed, I think spiritually therefore I am a spiritual being. Steiner's equation was that the spiritual activity of thinking is a proof statement of the reality of spirituality by the individual's direct experience of spiritual thinking. Spiritual thinking = spiritual existence. Each individual can have this experience. The individual spiritual activity proves the reality of the individual's spirit. Or as Christ stated, "Seek and you shall find" (Matt. 7:7). Dr. Steiner would add for our age, seek Christ and you shall find your true spiritual nature.

Steiner called this spiritual, or etheric, thinking "sense-free thinking," which opens to the spiritual nature of

43

thinking and, therefore, to the spiritual world and spiritual beings. Etheric thinking is organic, alive, and vibrant in contrast to sense-bound thinking, which is more like a corpse. Sense-bound thinking is the residue of real thinking.

Christ has returned in the etheric, spiritual realm. Therefore, we must be capable of etheric perception through etheric thinking. If we do not develop such etheric thinking, we will be spiritually blind to the second coming of Christ. Steiner's works were aimed at igniting this potential capacity in each individual to apprehend Christ.

The following excerpts are from Rudolf Steiner in his lecture course *The Gospel of St. John*, lecture 12: "The Nature of the Virgin Sophia and of the Holy Spirit." In these statements, he defined our path to Christ.

> If we permit what is written in the Gospel of John to work sufficiently upon us, our astral body is in the process of becoming a Virgin Sophia, and it will become receptive to the Holy Spirit. Gradually, through the strength of the impulse that emanates from this Gospel, it will become receptive to feeling, and later to perceiving, what is truly spiritual. This mission, this charge, was given to the writer of the Gospel by Jesus Christ. You need only read the Gospel. The Mother of Jesus—the Virgin Sophia, in the esoteric Christian sense—stands at the foot of the Cross, and from the Cross Christ says to the disciple whom He loved: "Behold thy mother! And from that hour that disciple took her unto his own home" (19:27). This means: The force that was in my astral body and made it capable of becoming bearer of the Holy Spirit, I now give over to you; you shall write down what this astral body has been able to acquire through its development! "And from that hour that disciple took her unto his own home"—this means that he wrote the Gospel of John. And this Gospel

of John is the Gospel in which the writer has concealed powers that develop the Virgin Sophia. At the Cross, he was entrusted with the mission of receiving that force as his mother and of being the true, genuine interpreter of the Messiah. This means that, if you live wholly in accordance with the Gospel of John and understand it spiritually, it has the force to lead you to Christian catharsis; it has the power to give you the Virgin Sophia. Then the Holy Spirit, united with the Earth, will grant you, in the Christian sense, illumination, or *photismos!*

What the most intimate disciples experienced there in Palestine was so powerful that, from that time on, they possessed at least the capacity to perceive the spiritual world. The most intimate disciples had received this capacity into themselves. Perceiving in the spirit in the Christian sense means that people transform their astral body to such a degree through the power of the event of Palestine that what they see does not need to be there externally, physically.

They possess something by means of which they can perceive in the spirit. There were such intimate pupils.*

The miracle of the Resurrection is to be taken quite literally. He conquered death and remains with us for He said: "Lo, I remain with you always, even unto the end of the age, unto the end of the cosmic age" (Matt. 28:20).

He is there and will come again, although not in a form of flesh but in a form in which those who have been sufficiently developed through the power of the Gospel of John can actually perceive Him, and, possessing the power to perceive Him, they will no longer be unbelieving. This is the mission of the anthroposophical movement: to prepare those who have the will to allow themselves to be prepared for the return of the Christ upon Earth. This is the

---

* Steiner, *The Gospel of John,* pp. 179–80.

world-historical significance of anthroposophical spiritual science: to prepare humanity and to keep its eyes open for the time when the Christ will appear again actively among us in the sixth cultural epoch, in order that what was indicated to us in the Marriage at Cana may be accomplished for a great part of humanity.

Therefore, the anthroposophical worldview appears like an execution of the testament of Christianity. In order to be led to real Christianity, the people of the future will have to receive that spiritual teaching that anthroposophy is able to give.*

Like Mary, we need an Immaculate Conception to bear Christ within us. We need catharsis to cleanse our souls. Like John the Baptist, we need to bear witness to the presence of Christ and make straight the paths to Lord. We need to stick to the essential. Like John the Evangelist we must listen to Mary's words at Cana, "Do whatever he tells you" (John 2:5). Like St. Francis, we need purging of our egotistical passions.

Beholding Christ

When we look at the *Sistine Madonna* by Raphael, we see a depiction of the mystery of incarnation. How does a spiritual being take on flesh? Through love. Mary lovingly holds Christ. She is also presenting Him to us.

The Marian way of beholding and bearing witness to the spiritual presence of Christ is the goal of the Gospel of St. John and Anthroposophy. Etheric thinking, a new heartfelt thinking, becomes the organ for this perception. Then each individual can, out of freedom, join with Mary in saying "Yes!"

---

* Ibid., pp. 182–83.

Raphael's Sistine Madonna (see frontispiece) was recaptured in Michelangelo's *Pietà*, which depicts the mystery of excarnation. Where did the spirit previously housed in the flesh go? Mary not only lovingly holds Christ; she is also presenting His sacrifice to the world. Mary is bearing Christ in both images. Through Mary, we behold and bear witness to Christ.

Pietà *(compassion), 1498–1499, by Michelangelo*
(St. Peter's Basilica, Vatican City)

MARIAN SITES

Because Mary was Jewish and raised in Israel, one would expect a large number of Marian shrines in Israel. The number of Marian sites in Israel moves us to realize the criticality of Mary to the Christ events. Mary makes Christ human and therefore more believable. These sites create love and a sense of reverence for this incredible woman. There are Marian sites all over the world, from Israel to Turkey to Ireland, France, Portugal and Mexico. Visiting her sites is extremely poignant.

The Galilee

Nazareth is in Galilee, where Jesus was raised by Mary and Joseph. The Israelis refer to the area as The Galilee, including the Sea of Galilee. Hebrew did not have words to differentiate the sizes of bodies of water. Anything bigger than a puddle was a sea. We would call them lakes.

The Sea of Galilee is one of the most peaceful places you can ever visit. Tranquility is its most striking attribute. It is surrounded by small hills and seems protected. The sea still has rich mineral deposits in its waters from nearby springs on the Northern side, and therefore has good fishing. It seems unchanged from when Christ walked its shores. Christ spent most of His ministry there. You can walk on sites where Christ most likely walked and talked. The sites include the

Church of the Mount of the Beatitudes, The Church of the Multiplication of Loaves and Fishes, and the Church where Christ prepared breakfast after His Resurrection.

As Emil Bock points out in his book *The Three Years,* Galilee is Eden-like in its nature. It has water and therefore vegetation and growth. The air is clear and sweet. It seems to be in eternal spring.

Galilee sits in direct contrast to the deserts and wilderness of Judea, and especially the city of Jerusalem. Jerusalem is high in the mountains, and you must travel through rough lands to get from Galilee to Jerusalem. It would take days to make this arduous pilgrimage on foot. For Christ it is a journey from life toward death.

It is easy to understand why Jesus preferred Galilee for the majority of His ministry. He started His ministry in Cana, where he also taught His disciples after His Resurrection. After three years, He ends His sojourn on earth by the Sea of Galilee. This place seems timeless. This is where Mary and Jesus spent most of their lives.

Church of The Annunciation, Nazareth

The Catholic Church of The Annunciation in Nazareth is a large modern church built around the grotto where, according to tradition, the house of Mary stood. This is the place where the Angel Gabriel appeared to Mary and announced that she was chosen as the maiden to give birth to The Messiah. It is the combination of the site with the often-read words that move you. This is the place where Mary said, "Yes" to do God's will! As is often the case, the Greek Orthodox do not agree with the Catholics that this was the actual site, and they have their site at what is called Mary's well. "And Mary said, Behold the handmaid of the

Lord; be it unto me according to thy word. And the angel departed from her" (Luke 1:38).

Church of the Visitation, Ein Kerem

This church is built on the site where Elizabeth and Zacharias lived and the home of their son, John the Baptist. Mary came to this site after the Angel Gabriel informed her that her cousin Elizabeth was pregnant. This is where the beautiful words of Elizabeth occurred about John leaping in her womb and Mary's glorious Magnificat was sung. "And it came to pass, that, when Elisabeth heard the salutation of Mary, the babe leaped in her womb; and Elisabeth was filled with the Holy Ghost" (Luke 1:41).

Church of The Nativity, Bethlehem

According to tradition, St. Helena found this site, and Anne Katherine Emmerich's inner experiences affirm St. Helena's discovery. This is one of the oldest continuously operating churches in the world. Beneath the church is the cave where Jesus was born. The spot is marked by a star and you can reach through a hole and touch the stone of the cave. Having tactile experiences, touching holy sites, is astounding. It is a startling experience to touch the stone of the cave where Jesus may have been born. From the cave of his birth to the cave of His resurrection, Christ's life forces seem inexplicably linked with bringing life out of the material stones of caves. Maybe in this sense he answers the devil's temptation to turn stones into bread (life). This site as a cave is very similar in atmosphere to the crypt where Christ was buried.

The Wedding Church, Cana

The site of Christ's first miracle was probably at or near the synagogue and a source of water. It is interesting that, from St. John's perspective, Mary was the instigator of His ministry and His first miracle with her famous words to the servants, "Whatever he saith unto you, do it" (John 2:5). This advice is appropriate down the ages and into the future. Similar words are uttered by God the Father at the Transfiguration, "Listen to him" (Matt. 17:5 ESV).

Golgotha

No site is so poignant as Golgotha, which includes the site of the Crucifixion, Christ's tomb, and the first sighting of Christ after His Resurrection. Here, Mary suffered the gory crucifixion and death of her beloved son. It is the site where she held him the last time, memorialized by Michelangelo in his *Pietà*. Here, her world seemed to end. Her heart was broken. Her catharsis was complete. She was duly prepared for Christ's triumphant Resurrection.

The Upper Room

The Upper Room may be the second most important Christian site after Golgotha. The Last Supper, which included the first communion, was celebrated here. The resurrected Christ became manifest to His apostles in the Upper Room. Mary prayed here with the Apostles after Christ's Ascension. Pentecost occurred here. It is also where Peter and the Apostles in danger of death, boldly preached the good news of Resurrection.

Basilica of Mary's Assumption, Jerusalem

This is the site where Mary fell asleep and passed to the other side. There are radically different assumptions on whether, like Christ, she experienced a sort of Ascension.

Mary's Home in Ephesus.

It is unclear whether Mary went with John to Ephesus. This would contradict the idea that she died in Jerusalem. It is mainly legend. If she did go to Ephesus, her death would have occurred here. Anne Katherine Emmerich had insights into Mary's home in Ephesus. Two priests excavated where she indicated the home of Mary would be, and they found what they believe is her final home. It is a sacred site in Turkey and the only place in a Muslim country that allows Catholic masses outside throughout the day for the large number of pilgrims. There is a wall of white petitions addressed to Mary. Muslims have a special affinity for Mary. Mary is the only woman named in the Quran.

MARIAN APPARITIONS

This is a subject that can become immediately suspect. Modern people demand a scientifically verifiable test to confirm the truth, which is hard to do with apparitions. Spiritual realities do not fit into a materialistic paradigm of lab apparatus; apparitions are difficult to quantify. The Roman Catholic Church is concerned with false or inaccurate visions that cannot be verified. The test of time is the best approach. It is noteworthy to observe the modesty and humility of the individuals involved, many of whom were very young and uneducated. Their innocence seems to be a key factor. What can be observed is the incredible reverence that individuals display at these sites. Millions of people go to them and pray.

One constant in many of these apparitions is that Mary is often described in words that are similar to her appearance in the Book of Revelation. "And there appeared a great wonder in heaven; a woman clothed with the sun, and the moon under her feet, and upon her head a crown of twelve stars" (Rev. 12:1).

At Fatima in Portugal, the children described Mary as "the Lady more brilliant than the Sun" (Wikipedia). She was observed as "a woman brighter than the sun, shedding rays of light clearer and stronger than a crystal goblet filled with the most sparkling water and pierced by the burning rays of the sun" (Wikipedia).

Mary often calls for prayer, especially of the rosary. Since many of the visionaries were illiterate, it gives pause to understand how they described something from *The Book of Revelation*. Many of the visionaries suffered because of their stories. Priests, politicians and even the mother of the Fatima children disbelieved them.

Our Lady of Guadalupe and Juan Diego

Gene Gollogly was the director of SteinerBooks and had a deep devotion to Mary. He had a contagious, enthusiastic nature, especially about the spiritual. Gene and I had numerous conversations regarding Mary. Gene, being Gene, flew to Mexico to visit the shrine of Our Lady of Guadalupe. The Basilica of Our Lady of Guadalupe in Mexico City is the most visited Catholic pilgrimage site in the Americas. The following is Gene's essay from the SteinerBooks Holiday Catalog of 2006.

OUR LADY OF GUADALUPE

Gene Gollogly

The Spaniards arrived in the New World in 1492 and eventually made their way to the heart of the Aztec Empire—what is today Mexico City.

According to legend, the Aztecs had left their lands to the south, led by divine instruction in search of an eagle, perched on a cactus, with a serpent in its mouth. They found the "sign" in a region of seven lakes, where they made their capital city and centered their empire.

When the Spaniards arrived at the capital, they found a religion based on the sacrifice of human lives through a blood offering. Cutting out the hearts of the sacrificed, the Aztecs sacrificed thousands of victims a year to their god, Quetzalcoatl, the feathered serpent. The Spanish stopped the practice, but did not stop the flow of blood. They, too, killed, tortured, and destroyed, but now in the name of Christianity to "save" souls and bring the true faith to the natives.

Don Nuño de Guzmán, who was notorious for his torture and killing of the indigenous peoples, was the head of the Spanish local Government in the New World. Conversion

was enforced at the point of the sword and came from a state of fear. The Franciscan Bishop, Fray Juan de Zumárraga, though a fervent evangelizer himself, sent secret letters to Emperor Charles V asking for a new civil authority that would be kinder to the Indians. He also prayed to the Virgin Mary for help and asked for Castilian roses as a sign that he was being heard. Paradoxically, Zumárraga was not only a great evangelizer (he boasted in a letter that he'd destroyed more than five hundred temples and twenty thousand idols); he was also a defender of the Indians. He wanted them to be alive so that he could convert them and save their souls and feared that the civil authority was killing them in such appallingly large numbers that the population would be decimated.

In the middle of the city of lakes stood the sacred hill of Tepeyac. On it was a temple dedicated to the goddess Tonantzin, meaning "Our Mother," the Aztec goddess of fertility. The goddess did not demand blood sacrifice. The Spanish invaders destroyed this temple, too, along with all the other temples, because it was not Christian. Moreover, they erected a Cross in place of Tonantzin's temple on top of the sacred hill of Tepeyac.

Among the local natives was one who had been converted. He was an Indian "peasant" who took the name Juan Diego. His original name in Nahuatl was Cuauhtlatohuac, meaning "he who speaks like an eagle." To be from Cuauhtlatohuac was to be of the noble order of the eagle. The eagle was the representative of the Sun, who was a god. Therefore, Juan Diego's name implies that he had some spiritual knowledge and was a messenger of the Sun, although to outer appearances he was simply a poor Indian.

On December 9, 1531, before dawn, Juan Diego set out from home and was crossing Tepeyac hill to go to Church. He heard birds singing on top of the hill in a beautiful choir— sounds and songs he had never heard before. Then he heard a voice calling out his name. He climbed to the top of the hill, where he saw a "beautiful lady" who spoke to him in Nahuatl, his native language. The story has been translated in a number of versions and is well worth meditating upon.

The Lady said, "Listen, my most abandoned son, dignified Juan: Where are you going?" Juan answered, "My Owner and My Queen, I have to go to your house of Mexico-Tlatelolco, to follow all the divine things that our priests, who are the images of our Lord, have given to us."

Then the Lady talked with him, unveiling her precious will. She told him: "Know and be certain in your heart, my most abandoned son, that I am the Ever-Virgin Holy Mary, Mother of the God of Great Truth, of the One through Whom We Live, the Creator of Persons, the Owner of What is Near and Together, of the Lord of Heaven and Earth."

Much happens then, but the essence is this: The Lady told Juan Diego to go and tell the bishop that a temple/sanctuary/church should be built on the hill Tepeyac and dedicated to her. Juan Diego dutifully went to the bishop and, after being abused by his servants and forced to wait a long time, was eventually granted an audience. He told the bishop his story and what the Lady had said to him, but naturally the bishop refused to believe an old Indian and had him thrown out.

Juan then returned to Tepeyac and told the Lady what had happened. The Lady said he would have to go again to the bishop the next day and then return and tell her what happened. Early the next morning, Juan Diego got up and went to see the bishop. After waiting a long time, he was again allowed to see the bishop and tell his story. Again, the bishop did not believe him and told him to bring back a sign if his story was true. Sadly, Juan Diego then returned home.

Arriving at home, he found his uncle Juan Bernardino gravely ill. Juan Diego stayed home to care for his uncle and missed the evening's appointment with the lady. He stayed home the next day, too, to care for his uncle, who suffered from smallpox. His uncle sensed he was dying, however, and begged Juan to get a priest for his confession. Juan went back to town to find a priest. As he passed Tepeyac hill again very early on the morning of the twelfth, the Lady floated down and told him his uncle was cured. She told him to go to the top of the hill, collect roses, and take them as a sign to the bishop. Juan went up to the hilltop and found many blooming, dew-covered roses. He gathered them in his cloak, a *tilma*,* and returned to see the bishop.

Again, Juan Diego had to endure a long wait and abuse from the bishop's servants. The bishop was meeting with the newly arrived governor of Mexico. Finally, however, Juan Diego was admitted for an audience. He opened up his *tilma* and spread the roses on the floor. Then something unimaginable happened. Suddenly, on the tilma, there was also the image of a Lady! Everyone was filled with awe and fell to their knees. The bishop was stunned. He alone knew that the roses were the sign that he had been asking for—and there, too, was the miraculous image!

Bishop Zumárraga believed and built the church as the "Lady" had asked. Juan told the bishop that the Lady had called herself "Tecoatlazopeu," which means the lady "who crushed Quetzalcoatl," the god who demanded human sacrifice. The Spaniards could not quite understand this name

---

* A *tilmàtli* was an Aztec outer garment for men, worn in front like a long apron and frequently used as a carryall or as a cloak wrapped around the shoulders. Several types were used for the various classes in society. Upper classes wore a tilma of cotton cloth knotted over the right shoulder, while the middle class used a tilma made of ayate fiber, a coarse fabric derived from the threads of the maguey cactus. It was knotted over the left shoulder. The lower classes knotted the garment behind the neck, where it could serve for carrying. The most famous tilmàtli was that worn by Juan Diego and preserved in the shrine of Our Lady of Guadalupe.

and therefore named the lady Guadalupe, after the Sanctuary of Guadalupe de Caceres in Extremadura, in southern Spain, where there is a sixth century "Black Virgin"—a wooden statue of Mary that is dark because of the wood from which she was made. Indeed, the phenomena of the Black Virgins is well worth studying.

Black Madonna of Montserrat

Juan Diego's uncle, Juan Bernardino, however, said that her name was Tlecuauh-tlacupeuh ("she who comes flying from the light like an eagle of fire"). Several variations of her name exist, including Tequantlaxopeuh ("she who banishes those that ate us") and Coatlaxopeuh ("she who crushed the serpent's head").

The native people of the Americas at that time understood a picture language, in both words and images. Both the story and the image convey important signs. The singing of the birds draws the indigenous people into a sacred space; the fact that the bird songs are so unusual and beautiful says something special is to come.

In the conversation between Our Lady and Juan Diego, she addresses him with respect "Juantzin, Juan Diegotzin"—the ending *tzin* means "you are worthy of respect." This indicates that the Lady respects all native peoples. The Lady respects them, speaks their language, and chooses one of their own to communicate to the conquerors and Church authorities.

Native peoples are accepted in their own reality. She does not get angry with Juan Diego when the bishop rejects him, but encourages him gently to try again. Juan Diego is able to talk naturally and endearingly with the Lady, and she listens and gives him wise counsel. She cures Juan Bernardino of the illness that the native peoples know all too well. The fact that the roses are covered with dew is also important. Dew is the healing essence of the flower for the soul and spirit. Many of the native peoples understood the properties of roses. They understood that they spoke to the heart. At the beginning of the story, Our Lady asks, "Where are you going?" This is a question that can be asked of all of us. Our Lady is then asking all of us to build a temple—not an outer building, but an inner sanctuary where we can meet her.

The image of Our Lady of Guadalupe revealed and reveals many things. She stands in front of a sun and is therefore greater than their sun god was. She stands on the moon, and therefore is more important than the moon god. A winged being holds her up, which means she is from the sky; but her hands are joined in prayer, which means there must be one greater than she. The bluish-green cover of her cloak is representative of kings, but her eyes are lowered, so she is bowing to someone else. The black sash beneath her breasts above her stomach means she is pregnant, so she is carrying a baby of royal blood. The white fur at the neck and the gold border were marks of royalty for the Aztecs. The stars on her cloak and the fact that she is being carried means that a new time was coming. She is framed by the rays of the sun in alternating patterns of curved and wide rays and straight and narrow rays. There are sixty-two on her right side, and seventy-seven on her left. (The seventy-seven rays are reminiscent of the number of generations before the Nathan Jesus child of Luke's Gospel.)

On her cloak are nine large, triangular Mexican magnolia flowers (reminiscent of the nine hierarchies). She has a Flower of the Sun—a single four-petalled flower over the child in the womb—which represents fulfillment. The cross-shaped flowers on her cloak are *mamalhuarztli,* which signify new life. The Mexican magnolias symbolize the beating hearts of victims of sacrifice, and as a pregnant woman is wearing them, her issue will be another but final victim. The Lady's left knee is slightly bent and because the triangular flowers also represent maracas (musical instruments), she is seen to be dancing for joy, The Lady's hair and skin color is dark and olive colored, close to that of the Native people of Central America (and of the Holy Land). Her racial facial features are not those of a Native person or a European, but suggest those of a Mestizo woman, the fruit of the mixing of European and Native peoples, prophetic of a new mixed race. Her hair is parted in the middle and worn under a mantle, a covering similar to the *rebozo* (a kind of multi-purpose shawl) worn by native Indian women. This cover was the color of the quetzal, a highland bird, whose feathers were valuable and used to denote nobility and sanctity.

In the early 1500s, Raphael painted many remarkable Madonnas. Many have studied these paintings and understand their unique beauty and wonderful picture language. In many of them, Raphael shows the hairstyle of Our Lady of Guadalupe. And in the Small Cowper Madonna (in the National Gallery in Washington, D.C.), the color of her cloak is similar to that of Guadalupe.

Our Lady appeared three times to Juan Diego. She also appeared to Juan Diego's uncle, Juan Bernardino, who recovered as he lay dying of smallpox.

Four is the sacred number for indigenous people everywhere. Four represents the four cardinal points and the elements of water, fire, air, and earth. (In some versions of the story, Juan Diego was turned away four times before he could see the bishop.)

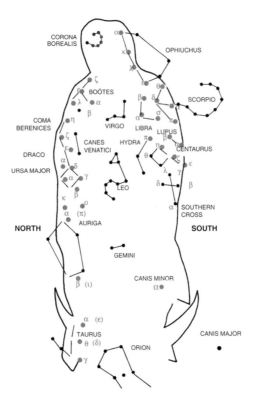

In a geographical sense, if Tepeyac Hill is the Flower of the Sun at the center, the nine flowers are positioned just where the surrounding mountains are. The winter solstice in 1531 took place on Tuesday, December 12th. The sky map for that date at 10:40 is on the tilma, with both the Northern constellations and the Southern ones clearly indicated through the position of the stars on the tilma.

San Juan Diego

Bishop Zumárraga erected the Church to "Our Lady of Guadalupe," and thousands of people came to see the image. The conversion of millions of native peoples to Christianity then occurred quickly, peacefully, in synchronicity with their spiritual understanding. Tilmas naturally decay after fifteen years or so, but this tilma has survived in perfect condition for nearly five hundred years. In 1660, the Roman Catholic Church named Our Lady of Guadalupe the "Mother of God," considering her synonymous with the Virgin Mary. She became the Patron Saint of Mexico. In 1921, a bomb placed in a flowerpot right under the tilma exploded and caused extensive structural damage to the church (now a cathedral), but the tilma survived untouched.

In 1945, Pope Pius XII designated Our Lady of Guadalupe "Empress of the Americas," from Eagle Alaska to Tierra del Fuego, North, Central, and South (that is, from the Eagle to the Fire). Endearingly, many Mexicans often call Our Lady of Guadeloupe "La Morenita," or Little Darkling.

Today, there is tremendous interest in Mary/Isis/Sophia. Even in New York City, last December hundreds of young people dressed in red, white, and blue track suits (from the red, white, and blue feathered wings of the supporting angel under Our Lady and symbolizing loyalty, faith, and fidelity) paraded with banners of Our Lady of Guadalupe and celebrated her feast day. The church that is dedicated to her in New York City (on 14th Street and 8th Avenue) is covered with large murals of her apparition to Juan Diego. On Sundays there, both English and Spanish masses are crowded, while other local churches have small attendance.

Our Lady of Guadalupe has also become the heart of "liberation theology." She is seen as the comforter of the oppressed, the downtrodden, the despairing, and the poor. She appears everywhere—at political events like the Caesar Chavez marches for the rights of farm workers in the 1960s and 1970s and at the recent marches for immigration reform in Los Angeles, Miami, Dallas, New York, and other cities. She is acknowledged throughout Latin America and by Native Americans in the United States.

While in New Mexico and Arizona, I was surprised at how often her image is seen not only in homes and churches, but also in sweat lodges and kivas. Most native peoples, including the Navajo and the Yaqui Indians I visited, show a devotion to Our Lady of Guadalupe and include her among their sacred ancestors.

Throughout the Americas, Our Lady of Guadalupe is not just an image, but is also a living presence.

The following essays are from Wikipedia. They are succinct summaries of the apparitions and avoid concerns over dogma. Unfortunately, Wikipedia is an ever-changing source of information and changes over time. Wikipedia's information should be considered illustrative, but not definitive.

Fatima in Portugal and the Three Children

In the spring and summer of 1916, nine-year-old Lúcia dos Santos and her cousins Francisco and Jacinta Marto were herding sheep at the Cova da Iria near their home village of Aljustrel the parish of Fátima, Portugal. They later said they were visited three times by an apparition of an angel. They said the angel, who identified himself as the "Angel of Peace" and "Guardian Angel of Portugal," taught them prayers, to make sacrifices, and to spend time in adoration of the Lord.

Beginning in the spring of 1917, the children reported apparitions of an Angel, and starting in May 1917, apparitions of the Virgin Mary, whom the children described as "the Lady more brilliant than the Sun." The children reported a prophecy that prayer would lead to an end to the Great War, and that on October 13th that year the Lady would reveal her identity and perform a miracle "so that all may believe." Newspapers reported the prophecies, and many pilgrims began visiting the area. The children's accounts were deeply controversial, drawing intense criticism from both local secular and religious authorities. A provincial administrator briefly took the children into custody, believing the prophecies were politically motivated in opposition to the officially secular First Portuguese Republic established in 1910. The events of October 13th became known as the Miracle of the Sun.

*Lúcia dos Santos (right) with her cousins
Francisco and Jacinta Marto, 1917*

On May 13, 1917, the children reported seeing a woman "brighter than the sun, shedding rays of light clearer and stronger than a crystal goblet filled with the most sparkling water and pierced by the burning rays of the sun." The woman wore a white mantle edged with gold and held a rosary in her hand. She asked them to devote themselves to the Holy Trinity and to pray "the Rosary every day, to bring peace to the world and an end to the war." While the children had never told anyone about seeing the angel, Jacinta told her family about seeing the brightly lit woman. Lúcia had earlier said that the three should keep this experience private. Jacinta's disbelieving mother told neighbors about it as a joke, and within a day the whole village knew of the children's vision.

The children said that the woman told them to return to the Cova da Iria on June 13, 1917. Lúcia's mother sought counsel from the parish priest, Father Ferreira, who suggested she allow them to go. He asked to have Lúcia brought to him afterward so that he could question her. The second appearance occurred on June 13th, the feast of Saint Anthony, patron of the local parish church. On this occasion, the lady revealed that Francisco and Jacinta would be taken to Heaven soon, but Lúcia would live longer in order to spread her message and devotion to the Immaculate Heart of Mary.

During the June visit, the children said the lady told them to say the Holy Rosary daily in honor of Our Lady of the Rosary to obtain peace and the end of the Great War. (On April 21st, the first contingent of Portuguese soldiers had embarked for the front lines of the war.) The lady also purportedly revealed to the children a vision of hell, and entrusted a secret to them, described as "good for some and bad for others." Fr. Ferreira later stated that Lúcia recounted that the lady told her, "I want you to come back on the thirteenth and to learn to read in order to understand what I want of you.... I don't want more."

In the following months, thousands of people flocked to Fátima and nearby Aljustrel, drawn by reports of visions and miracles. On August 13, 1917, the provincial administrator Artur Santos (no relation to Lúcia dos Santos) intervened, as he believed that these events were politically disruptive in the conservative country. He took the children into custody, jailing them before they could reach the Cova da Iria. Santos interrogated and threatened the children to get them to divulge the contents of the secrets. Lúcia's mother hoped the officials could persuade the children to end the affair and admit that they had lied. Lúcia told Santos everything short of the secrets, and offered to ask the woman for permission to tell the official the secrets.

That month, instead of the usual apparition in the Cova da Iria on August 13, the children reported that they saw the Virgin Mary on August 19, a Sunday, at nearby Valinhos, Fátima. She asked them again to pray the Rosary daily, spoke about the miracle coming in October, and asked them "to pray a lot, a lot for the sinners and sacrifice a lot, as many souls perish in hell because nobody is praying or making sacrifices for them."

The three children claimed to have seen the Blessed Virgin Mary in a total of six apparitions between May 13 and October 13, 1917. Lúcia also reported a seventh Marian apparition at Cova da Iria. 2017 marked the hundredth anniversary of the apparitions.

Miracle of the Sun

After some newspapers reported that the Virgin Mary had promised a miracle for the last of her apparitions on October 13th, a huge crowd, possibly between 30,000 and

100,000, including reporters and photographers, gathered at Cova da Iria. What happened then became known as the "Miracle of the Sun."

Various claims have been made as to what actually happened during the event. The three children who originally claimed to have seen Our Lady of Fátima reported seeing a panorama of visions during the event, including those of Jesus, Our Lady of Sorrows, Our Lady of Mount Carmel, and of Saint Joseph blessing the people. Father John De Marchi, an Italian Catholic priest and researcher wrote several books on the subject, which included descriptions by witnesses who believed they had seen a miracle created by Mary, Mother of God. According to accounts, after a period of rain, the dark clouds broke and the Sun appeared as an opaque, spinning disc in the sky. It was said to be significantly duller than normal, and to cast multicolored lights across the landscape, the people, and the surrounding clouds. The Sun was then reported to have careened towards the Earth before zigzagging back to its normal position. Witnesses reported that their previously wet clothes became "suddenly and completely dry, as well as the wet and muddy ground that had been previously soaked because of the rain that had been falling."

Lourdes in France and Bernadette Soubirous

By the time of the events at the grotto, the Soubirous family's financial and social status had declined to the point where they lived in a one-room basement, formerly used as a jail called Le Cachot (the dungeon), where they were housed at no charge by her mother's cousin, André Sajoux.

On February 11, 1858, Soubirous, then aged fourteen, was out gathering firewood with her sister Toinette and a friend near the grotto of Massabielle (Tuta de Massavielha), when she experienced her first vision. While the other girls crossed the little stream in front of the grotto and walked on, Soubirous stayed behind, looking for a place to cross where she wouldn't get her stockings wet. She finally sat down to take her shoes off to cross the water and was lowering her stocking when she heard the sound of rushing wind, but nothing moved. A wild rose in a natural niche in the grotto, however, did move. From the niche, or rather the dark alcove behind it, "came a dazzling light, and a white figure." This was the first of eighteen visions of what she referred to as *aquero,* Gascony Occitan meaning "that." In later testimony, she called it "a small young lady" (*uo petito damizelo*). Her sister and her friend stated that they had seen nothing.

On February 14th, following Sunday Mass, Soubirous and her sister Marie and other girls returned to the grotto. Soubirous knelt immediately, saying she saw the apparition again. When one of the girls threw holy water at the niche and another threw a rock from above that shattered on the ground, the apparition disappeared. On her next visit, February 18th, Soubirous said that "the vision" asked her to return to the grotto every day for a fortnight.

This period of almost daily visions came to be known as *la Quinzaine sacrée,* "holy fortnight." Initially, Soubirous's parents, especially her mother, were embarrassed and tried to forbid her to go. The supposed apparition did not identify herself until the seventeenth vision. Although the townspeople who believed she was telling the truth assumed she saw the Virgin Mary, Soubirous never claimed it to be Mary, consistently using the word *aquerò.* She described the lady as wearing a white veil, a blue girdle and with a yellow rose on each foot—compatible with "a description of any statue of the Virgin in a village church."

Soubirous's story caused a sensation with the townspeople, who were divided in their opinions on whether or not she was telling the truth. Some believed her to have a mental illness and demanded she be put in an asylum.

The other contents of Soubirous's reported visions were simple and focused on the need for prayer and penance. On February 25th, she explained that the vision had told her "to drink of the water of the spring, to wash in it and to eat the herb that grew there" as an act of penance. To everyone's surprise, the next day the grotto was no longer muddy but clear water flowed. On March 2nd, at the thirteenth of the alleged apparitions, Soubirous told her family that the lady said that "a chapel should be built and a procession formed."

Soubirous's sixteenth claimed vision, which she stated went on for more than an hour, was on March 25th. According to her account, during that visitation, she again asked the woman for her name but the lady just smiled back. She repeated the question three more times and finally heard the lady say, in Gascon Occitan, "I am the Immaculate Conception" (*Qué soï era immaculado councepcioŭ*, a phonetic transcription of *Que soy era immaculada conceptiou*). Despite being rigorously interviewed by officials of both the Catholic Church and the French government, she stuck consistently to her story.

Results of her visions

In the 160 years since Soubirous dug up the spring, seventy cures have been verified by the Lourdes Medical Bureau as "inexplicable"—after what the Catholic Church claims are "extremely rigorous scientific and medical examinations" that failed to find any other explanation. The Lourdes Commission that examined Bernadette after the visions ran an intensive analysis on the water and found that, while it had a high mineral content, it contained nothing out of the ordinary that would account for the cures attributed to it. Bernadette said that it was faith and prayer that cured the sick: "One must have faith and pray; the water will have no virtue without faith."

Soubirous's request to the local priest to build a chapel at the site of her visions eventually gave rise to a number of chapels and churches at Lourdes. The Sanctuary of Our Lady of Lourdes is now one of the major Catholic pilgrimage sites in the world. One of the churches built at the site, the Basilica of St. Pius X, can accommodate 25,000 people and was dedicated by the future Pope John XXIII when he was the Papal Nuncio to France. Nearly five million pilgrims from all over the world visit Lourdes (population of about 15,000) every year to pray and to drink the miraculous water, believing that they obtain from the Lord healing of the body and of the spirit.

Later years

Disliking the attention she was attracting, Bernadette went to the hospice school run by the Sisters of Charity of Nevers, where she learned to read and write. Although she considered joining the Carmelites, her health precluded her entering any of the strict contemplative orders. On July 29, 1866, with forty-two other candidates, she took the religious habit of a postulant and joined the Sisters of Charity at their motherhouse at Nevers. Her Mistress of Novices was Sister Marie Therese Vauzou. The Mother Superior at the time gave her the name Marie-Bernarde in honor of her god-mother, who was named "Bernarde."

Bernadette in 1866, after having taken the religious habit of the Sisters of Charity

Patricia A. McEachern observes, "Bernadette was devoted to Saint Bernard, her patron saint; she copied long texts related to him in notebooks and on bits of paper. The experience of becoming "Sister" Marie-Bernard marked a turning point for Bernadette, as she realized more than ever that the great grace she received from the Queen of Heaven brought with it great responsibilities."*

Soubirous spent the rest of her brief life at the mother-house, working as an assistant in the infirmary and later as

---

* McEachern, *A Holy Life: The Writings of St. Bernadette of Lourdes.*

a sacristan, creating beautiful embroidery for altar cloths and vestments. Her contemporaries admired her humility and spirit of sacrifice. One day, asked about the apparitions, she replied, "The Virgin used me as a broom to remove the dust. When the work is done, the broom is put behind the door again."

Soubirous had followed the development of Lourdes as a pilgrimage shrine while she still lived at Lourdes but was not present for the consecration of the Basilica of the Immaculate Conception there in 1876.

Medjugorje in Croatia and the Six Children

Since 1981, when six local children said they had seen visions of the Blessed Virgin Mary, Medjugorje has become an unsanctioned destination of Catholic pilgrimage.

"Our Lady of Medjugorje" is the title given to the apparition by those who believe that Mary, mother of Jesus, has been appearing from June 24, 1981, until today to six children, now adults, in Medjugorje (then part of communist Yugoslavia). "Most Blessed Virgin Mary," "Queen of Peace," and "Mother of God" are terms with which the apparition has allegedly introduced herself.

The visionary Marija (Pavlović) Lunetti claims to receive messages from the Virgin Mary on the twenty-fifth of every month, while Mirjana (Dragičević) Soldo reports receiving messages on the second of the month.

The messages attributed to Our Lady of Medjugorje have a strong following among Catholics worldwide. Medjugorje has become one of the most popular pilgrimage sites for Catholics in the world and has turned into Europe's third most important apparition site, where each year more than 1 million people visit. It has been estimated that thirty million pilgrims have come to Medjugorje since the reputed apparitions began in 1981. Many have reported visual phenomena including the sun spinning in the sky or changing color and figures such as hearts and crosses around the sun. Some visitors have suffered eye damage while seeking to experience such phenomena. Jesuit Father Robert Faricy has written about his own experience of such phenomena, saying, "Yet I have seen rosaries that have changed color, and I have looked directly at the sun in Medjugorje and have seen it seem to spin and turn different colors. It would be easier to report that it is just hysteria except that I would then have to accuse myself of being hysterical, which I was not and am not."

Official Position of the Catholic Church

On August 21, 1996, Vatican Press Office spokesman Joaquin Navarro-Valls declared that Catholics may still travel on pilgrimage to Medjugorje and that priests may accompany them. Navarro-Valls declared: "You cannot say people cannot go there until it has been proven false. This has not been said, so anyone can go if they want."

A Vatican commission to study the Medjugorje question was set up by Pope Benedict XVI in 2010; headed by Cardinal Camillo Ruini, it was reported on January 18, 2014, to have completed its work, to be communicated to the Congregation for the Doctrine of the Faith. Pope Francis commented on the report as "very, very good" on May 13, 2017, when speaking to journalists. According to Italian media, the Ruini report divided the investigation into three main parts: the early apparitions from June 24, 1981, to July 3, 1981, the acclaimed apparitions thereafter, and the pastoral situation. The commission's findings were positive towards recognizing the supernatural nature of the first appearances and rejected the hypothesis of a demonic origin of the apparitions. But it could not reach a finding on the reported subsequent apparitions, despite a majority of the commission recognizing the spiritual benefits that Medjugorje had brought to pilgrims, including Pope Francis who remarked: "The third, the core of the Ruini report, the spiritual fact, the pastoral fact. People go there and convert. People who encounter God, change their lives…but this…there is no magic wand there. And this spiritual and pastoral fact can't be ignored."

On February 11, 2017, Pope Francis appointed Archbishop Henryk Hoser, S.A.C., the Bishop of Praga (in Warsaw), as Special Envoy of the Holy See to Medjugorje. By the end of 2017, Hoser had announced that the Vatican's position was in favor of organizing pilgrimages. "Today, dioceses and other institutions can organize official pilgrimages. It's no longer a problem," explained Archbishop Hoser. "Pope Francis [even] recently asked an Albanian cardinal to give his blessing to the faithful at Medjugorje." "I am full of admiration for the work the Franciscans are doing there," the Polish archbishop reported. "With a relatively small team—there are only a dozen of them—they do a huge job of welcoming pilgrims. Every summer they organize a youth festival. This year, there were 50,000 young people from around the world, with more than 700 priests."

He also cited the large number of confessions, adding, "There is a massive number of confessions. They have about fifty confessionals, which are not enough." "This is a phenomenon. And what confirms the authenticity of the place is the large number of charitable institutions that exist around the sanctuary. And another aspect, as well;

the great effort that is being made at the level of Christian formation. Each year, they organize conferences at different levels, for various audiences," exemplifying priests, doctors, parents, young people, and couples. "The decree of the former episcopal conference of what used to be Yugoslavia, which, before the Balkan war, advised against pilgrimages in Medjugorje organized by bishops, is no longer relevant," he said.

"Whatever he saith unto you, do it."
JOHN 2:5

Bibliography

Bock, Emil. *The Three Years: The Life of Christ between Baptism and Ascension.* Edinburgh, UK: Floris Books, 2005.

Emerson, Ralph Waldo. *Collected Works: Nature Addresses and Lectures,* rev. ed. Boston: Riverside, 1883.

Joyce, James. *A Portrait of the Artist as a Young Man.* New York: Viking, 1916.

Gardner, John Fentress. *The Experience of Knowledge.* New York: The Myrin Institute, 1962.

Levertov, Denise. *A Door in the Hive.* "Annunciation." New York, NY: New Directions, 1989.

McEachern, Patricia. *A Holy Life: The Writings of St. Bernadette of Lourdes.* San Francisco: Ignatius Press, 2005.

Morey, Sylvester M. *Native Americans and Our Way of Life.* Garden City, NY: The Myrin Institute, 1961.

Prokofieff, Sergei O. *Anthroposophy and the Philosophy of Freedom: Anthroposophy and Its Method of Cognition.* Forest Row, UK: Temple Lodge, 2009.

———. *The Heavenly Sophia and the Being Anthroposophia.* Forest Row, UK: Temple Lodge, 1996.

Reif Hughes, Gertrude. "Rudolf Steiner's Activist Epistemology and Feminist Thought in America." In *American Philosophy and Rudolf Steiner Emerson–Thoreau–Peirce–James–Royce–Dewey–Whitehead–Feminism* (ed. R. McDermott). Great Barrington, MA: Lindisfarne Books, 2012.

Reilly, Neill. *Songs and Dreams: By Seeking We Are Found.* Great Barrington, MA: Lindisfarne Books, 2017.

Smith, Edward Reaugh. *The Burning Bush: Rudolf Steiner, Anthroposophy, and the Holy Scriptures: Terms and Phrases.* Hudson, NY: Anthroposophic Press, 2001.

Steiner, Rudolf. *Awakening to Community* (CW 257, trans. M. Spock). Great Barrington, MA: SteinerBooks, 1973.

———. *The Festivals and their Meaning* (trans. rev. M. Barton). Forest Row, UK: Rudolf Steiner Press, 1996.

———. *The Gospel of John* (CW 103, trans. M. B. Monges; rev. F. Amrine). Great Barrington, MA: SteinerBooks, 2022.

———. *Isis Mary Sophia: Her Mission and Ours* (ed. C. Bamford). Great Barrington, MA: SteinerBooks, 2002.

———. *Knowledge of the Higher Worlds and its Attainment* (CW 10, trans. G. Metaxa). New York: Anthroposophic Press, 1947.

———. *Necessity and Freedom* (CW 166, trans. P. Wehrle). Hudson, NY: Anthroposophic Press, 1988.

———. *The Fifth Gospel: From the Akashic Record* (CW 148, trans. A. R. Meuss). Forest Row, UK: Rudolf Steiner Press, 1985.

———. *The Michael Mystery* (CW 26, trans. M. Spock). Great Barrington, MA: SteinerBooks, 1984, reprint, 2015.

———. *The Philosophy of Freedom: The Basis for a Modern World Conception* (CW 4, trans. M. Wilson). Forest Row, UK: Rudolf Steiner Press, 2011.

———. *Verses and Meditations* (trans. G. Adams and M. Adams). Forest Row, UK: Rudolf Steiner Press, 2004.

von Halle, Judith. *And if He has not been raised…: The Stations of Christ's Path to Spirit Man*. Trans. B. Strevens. Forest Row, UK: Temple Lodge, 2007.

Winkler, Franz E. *Man: The Bridge between Two Worlds*. New York: Harper and Row, 1960.

About the Author

Neill Reilly was born and raised on Long Island, New York. He graduated from Bowdoin College with a B.A. in Philosophy and from The Waldorf Institute at Adelphi University with an M.A. in Waldorf Pedagogy. Neill taught high school English for seven years at the Kimberton and Garden City Waldorf schools and at a Catholic high school and coached basketball, track, and lacrosse and directed plays. Following his work as a teacher, he began a career as a salesperson at Merrill Lynch, Lehman Brothers, Jefferies and Company, as well as numerous financial technology firms including EJV, NEON, and TIBCO. He is married with two children. Neill is also the author of *Songs and Dreams: By Seeking We Are Found* (Lindisfarne Books, 2017) and *Look at What We Can Become: Portraits of Five Michaelic Individuals* (SteinerBooks, 2019).

Songs and Dreams

By Seeking We Are Found

There is a correlation between waking experiences in a sleep state and inner experiences in a waking state. Both involve awakened consciousness. The songs in this volume are halting attempts to put into words inner events that are experienced in a waking consciousness. Inner experiences are filtered into images, ideas, and feelings, which are then translated into words. This derivative process condenses activity into words.

The polar opposite process must happen for you, the reader. If these words resonate when read, they then recreate images, ideas, and feelings. In this way, it is possible for the writer and the reader to experience a very similar inner activity. The creative process of each reader has a life of its own. Ironically, as individuals we create our own unique inner activity, which can lead to a universal experience.

ISBN 9781584209621 | pbk | 146 pages

Look at What We Can Become
Portraits of Five Michaelic Individuals

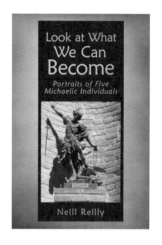

The term *Michaelic* refers to the qualities expressed by the Archangel Michael, who fights the dark forces that work to suppress human hope, goodness, loving kindness, and true community. Michael is often depicted as armored and resolute, giving no quarter to evil. He is intimately connected with Christ as Earth's guiding light. Each of these five individuals represents well-lived, Michaelic lives.

The five "Michaelic" individuals portrayed are Professor Fritz Koelln, John Fentress Gardner, Lee Lecraw, Marjorie Spock, and William Ward. As students of Rudolf Steiner's Spiritual Science, they each sought to bring new light to philosophy, education, and the arts for the future.

ISBN 9781621482468 | pbk | 124 pages